the everyday witch's coven

About the Author

Deborah Blake is the author of over a dozen books on modern Witchcraft, including *The Eclectic Witch's Book of Shadows*, *The Little Book of Cat Magic*, and *Everyday Witchcraft*, as well as the acclaimed *Everyday Witch Tarot* and *Everyday Witch Oracle*. She has also written three paranormal romance and urban fantasy series for Berkley, and her new cozy mystery series launched with *Furbidden Fatality* in 2021. Deborah lives in a 130-year-old farmhouse in upstate New York with numerous cats who supervise all her activities, both magical and mundane.

The Everyday Witch's

Coven

Rituals and Magic for Two or More

Deborah Blake

Llewellyn Publications
Woodbury, Minnesota

FIRST EDITION
First Printing, 2023

Book design by Rebecca Zins
Cover design by Cassie Willett
Cover illustration by Elizabeth Alba

Portions of this book were previously published in
Circle, Coven & Grove (Llewellyn, 2007)

Library of Congress Cataloging-In-Publication Data
Pending
ISBN 978-0-7387-7159-5

Llewellyn Publications
A Division of Llewellyn Worldwide Ltd.
2143 Wooddale Drive
Woodbury, MN 55125-2989

www.llewellyn.com
Printed in the United States of America

★ contents ★

Introduction

When I wrote *Circle, Coven & Grove: A Year of Magickal Practice* in 2005, it was my first book and I had been leading my group, Blue Moon Circle, since the spring of 2004. I primarily wrote it because it was the book I wished I had had when I was starting out as the leader of a new coven, with a year's worth of rituals for new moons, full moons, and sabbats, as well as some basic tools and advice. It was based on our own practice, and the rituals in the book were ones that I had created for us to use. Because my first high priestess had been Wiccan, the book and the rituals within it were fairly Wiccan in approach. This isn't a bad thing, mind you. It worked for us at the time and often still does, but that was then.

Now it is 2022. The face of modern Witchcraft is changing constantly, and many witches who are interested in practicing with others are not attracted to the Gardnerian style of Wicca with a high priest and high priestess, initiations and levels. Many of them don't want anything formal at all—they just want to belong to some kind of coven. From the emails and messages I get, I can see that many are searching for groups and unable to find one or are interested in starting their own but don't know where to start.

Many of the people I know who *do* practice with others are doing so in ways that are very different from the traditional coven. My friend Lisa has one friend with whom she does ritual at every sabbat—just the two of them. My daughter Jenn has a group of friends who get together for rituals periodically with whichever folks are available at the time, but they have no organized circle or leader (although she usually facilitates). Blue Moon Circle and I periodically go to a Beltane celebration put on by a larger group that combines their core members with visitors who have been brought in by someone who has been before (at least for their first time) and who can attend on their own from then on.

My own group practice has changed over the years as well. Blue Moon Circle still exists, over eighteen years later, and includes the same three core members who started it, as well as another longtime member and a couple of newer ones. But we've fluctuated from three to more than a dozen and back down again. We spent some time being open to new folks, then changed our minds and went back to being closed except under rare circumstances. We have turned out to be an all-women group, although that wasn't intentional, and decided we liked it that way.

I no longer refer to myself as a Wiccan high priestess, as I did back in the beginning, because our practice has become more eclectic and less classically Wiccan, and after all these years we are equals, even if I usually write the rituals. We stopped meeting on new moons almost entirely and are more likely to gather for sabbats and do full moons on our own due to a combination of scheduling issues and members getting older and not being able to drive at night. Sometimes practical conditions have to overrule our spiritual goals—that's another thing I've learned over all these years.

It occurred to me, the last couple of times I was asked about group practice, that I would no longer recommend *Circle, Coven & Grove* as a go-to book on covens, at least not for everyone. (Although the rituals still work just fine under most circumstances, and people still seem to get a lot out of it.) I needed a new book aimed at today's more eclectic witches, many of whom might not be in a position or have the desire for what we once considered to be a coven.

And so, like the first time, I decided to write the book I wished I had. *The Everyday Witch's Coven: Rituals and Magic for Two or More* encompasses everything I've learned in over eighteen years of leading a group. While it is suitable for more traditional Wiccans, it will also fulfill the needs of the eclectic witch—who is looking for an alternative to the more conventional approach to group practice—and everyone in between. Whether for two or twenty, those who want to practice on a regular basis with a committed group or occasionally with a friend or friends, this is a book for the modern witch.

section 1

the basics of a group practice

So you've decided that Witchcraft is the spiritual path for you, or else you have been practicing as a witch for a while and you're yearning to share that practice with others of like mind. Maybe it is time to join a coven. Maybe it is even time to start one of your own. But where do you start?

I suggest you begin by asking yourself some basic questions. These apply both if you are considering joining an existing group or trying to create one from scratch.

Are you starting a new coven or formalizing an existing one?

There is a lot to consider when you are starting a new group or formalizing an existing bunch of people into a more cohesive whole. Many of these questions are also good things to ask yourself if you are thinking of joining a preexisting group and wondering if it is the right place for you.

You don't necessarily need to have all the answers on day one, but it is a good idea to make sure that everyone involved is on the same page (or at least reading from the same book!) before you make a commitment to a long-term spiritual practice together.

Depending on the natures of the people taking part, you might end up winging it and seeing what happens. But if you are really starting from scratch, these are some of the issues you may want to discuss before you spend a lot of time and energy creating something just to discover it only works for half of those involved or possibly even disappoints everyone.

Just as with any other endeavor involving more than one person, good communication is key to success.

How many and how often?

These are two of the most vital questions to start with when forming a group: How large a group do you want, and how often do you want to meet? If you can't agree on these points, there are definitely going to be issues moving forward.

You may already know the answer to the first one if you are practicing with one or two other people and don't have any intention of expanding your circle to include others. Or, like some groups, you may be a loose collection of like-minded folks and are happy to include anyone who shows up whenever you do a ritual.

When Blue Moon Circle started out, we had three core members, but there were also a number of witches I'd practiced with in my first group, plus witchy people I knew from the local community, and we would invite any of them who wanted to join us for our larger sabbat rituals. For our first few years, this meant there was a regular but ever-changing bunch of folks taking part, and we might have anywhere from six to sixteen. Full moon rituals, however, we reserved for those who belonged to our own circle since they were more intimate and intense.

Eventually, however, we all decided that we wanted something more committed and less dependent on the whims of those who might or might not show up, so we stopped inviting those not in the group except under certain circumstances. We went, in essence, from being an "open" circle (one where anyone was welcome) to being a "closed" one (restricted to existing members and invited guests).

There were exceptions, of course. Sometimes one of us would have a friend who expressed interest in learning more about Witchcraft or someone with witchy leanings would find me through one of my books and ask to attend a ritual. I don't mind well-intentioned curiosity—after all, I didn't know I was a witch until I was invited to my first ritual and found out that Witchcraft was the spiritual path I'd been looking for all along—and the more people who can learn that witches are just like everyone else, the better.

We occasionally acquired a new member in this fashion, but the group agreed early on that new people would only be accepted after they had attended a few rituals to see if they fit in, and then only if everyone already in Blue Moon Circle agreed. Our numbers went up and down over the years as members came and went, but in the end, we ended up with our original core group plus one person who had also been attending since the beginning (but hadn't been sure she was a witch), and we stayed like that for a long time. It has only been in the last year that we added two new people, one of whom was a temporary housemate I acquired at the beginning of the pandemic. Good thing she turned out to be a witch!

For Blue Moon Circle, it took us quite a while to figure it out, but smaller and more intimate worked best for us. That may or may not be what works for you, but as a group, you should probably start out with a general agreement on the following points and be willing to adjust over time if the way you started out doesn't work for everyone.

How many people?

Do you want small and intimate, large and all-inclusive, or something in the middle? If not everyone wants the same thing, this may be an area that requires compromise. For instance, we had a couple of members who didn't care about size, I had a slight preference for larger, and one member had a strong preference for smaller.

So we eventually went with smaller, and I occasionally went to a larger ritual given by someone else. For us, that has worked the best. (And in time I came to want smaller too, so it all turned out fine.)

Who can invite new people to attend?

Only the person running the group (if there is one)? Anyone? Anyone but only if all those involved agree? You'll definitely want to discuss this ahead of time, especially if there are members in your group who are still in the broom closet and don't necessarily want strangers to know they are a witch.

Do the people attending have to be someone you know already or can strangers come?

Some open groups will post ritual times on a public board and anyone who wants can show up. Others will allow strangers if they are vouched for by someone already in the group. Some covens will allow guests only if they are someone a group member knows well.

Are you only interested in people who are experienced in a Witchcraft practice or are you willing to explain how everything works and lead new folks through the ritual?

There's more detailed discussion about this later, but it is an important point. Teaching newbie witches is a major commitment, and it changes the energy of the coven. Neither of these things is necessarily bad, but they are something to consider.

How often do you want to meet up?

This will vary from coven to coven depending both on what everyone wants from a group practice and what their schedules will allow. The first group I belonged to met on Thursdays every week and sometimes also on sabbats (holidays). The high priestess who ran it called it a study group rather than a coven, and her focus was on teaching and practice.

When I started Blue Moon Circle, we met on the sabbats and the full moons and new moons. Over the years, our lives have gotten busy and our schedules complicated, so we usually only manage to get together on the eight sabbats and sometimes on some occasion in between. We've given up on new moons entirely.

There is no "right" amount of times, just what works the best for the people in your coven. If you have some people who are dedicated to the group but can only make it once in a while, that's fine too, as long as everyone agrees that's acceptable.

Where will you gather?

There are various options for gathering places, but where your particular coven meets up will depend on a variety of issues, some of which may be out of your control.

For instance, depending on where you live, there may be public spaces you can use. Some Unitarian Universalist churches have a CUUPS chapter (Covenant of Unitarian Universalist Pagans) or are willing to start one. My former high priestess attended our local UU church and they allowed her to use their space for rituals. We actually did a number of public rituals there, which is great if you have a group that is open to anyone. I led a ritual at Yule one year that had over fifty people attending. That would never have worked in someone's house!

You might also be able to use a room at a sympathetic store, such as a Pagan/New Age shop or a local health food store. Sometimes those kinds of places have back rooms they are willing to let groups use or rent. Libraries and community centers often have rooms to rent or for free too.

There are also outdoor public spaces such as parks and forests. The first ritual I ever went to was held in a local park that happened to be next to the high priestess's house. It was a beautiful setting and surprisingly private since it was after dark on Samhain (Halloween). Apparently a bicycle cop stopped by at one point to see what all these strange people were up to and stayed to observe for a while. Most of us, me included, were so engrossed in the ritual that we never ever realized he was there.

If you are using a public space, keep in mind that there may be rules that prohibit open flames, whether candles or bonfires, and that in outdoor settings, like the one we were in, you will have no control over who wanders by. If that isn't an issue and you don't have another good place to meet, these options are well worth exploring. As witches, being outside can be a plus, especially on full moon nights.

Alternately, you may choose to meet someplace more private. Most covens gather at the home of one of their members, often that of whomever is leading the group. Some groups take turns meeting up at different people's houses, which can take the pressure off of one particular member to always clean and organize their space, not to mention setting up for the ritual.

Blue Moon Circle usually meets at my house, in part because I have a nice outside ritual space behind the barn to use when the weather permits (which in New York State isn't all that often) and enough room inside if we have to stay in. My house is also rural and very private, which is a bonus when we're dancing and chanting around a bonfire.

We have, however, come together at other member's houses if one of them wanted to host the ritual, and we've had feasts (with no obvious witchy undertones) at the home of one of our members whose husband likes the people in the group but isn't comfortable with Witchcraft.

A couple of things to keep in mind when you're deciding where you're going to meet:

- Is everyone in the group comfortable with being in public and acknowledging openly that they are a witch? If there are members of your group who are still in the broom closet, especially if they have sensitive jobs or prejudiced family members that would make being outed problematic, you will need to find someplace private. (I'm fortunate to live in a fairly accepting area, but there are some places in the United States and some other countries where Witchcraft is completely misunderstood. In these circumstances, public gatherings may not be an option.)
- If any of the people in your coven share their home with others, they will have to consider whether that person or persons will be comfortable having a magical gathering take place. If there are children, will there be

activities that are inappropriate or confusing to them? Sometimes you can get around this issue by holding your rituals when your kids / roommate / significant other / disapproving parents are out of the house. But if you can't, then it is probably best to meet up elsewhere.

- If there is more than one member with a home that will work, do you want to always come together at the same place or do you want to take turns? There are benefits either way, so this is mostly just a matter of what you choose to do. Practicing in the same space every time can be comfortable, and any place that is used repeatedly for magical work will eventually take on some powerful energy. On the other hand, it can be fun to take turns hosting, and it may be less effort if you share the burden. Again, this is something to discuss as you are starting a group practice, but keep in mind that you can always try it one way and switch to the other if it isn't working out.
- If you decide to practice outside, whether in a reasonably private public space, like a forest or a secluded park, or at someone's home, keep in mind that there is always the chance you will be seen (so if you intend to do your magical work *skyclad*, or naked, you will need to be cautious about where you choose). There will also be considerations such as weather, bugs, people's allergies, and the like. It is usually a good idea to have an indoor space as backup just in case the weather forecast for clear skies turns to torrential rain instead. I am a big proponent of having rituals outside whenever possible to connect with the land, the moon, and the rest of nature. But I assure you, in the middle of an upstate New York winter, we will be in my living room, not in my backyard. Also

> consider the conditions if you intend to have any kind of fire outside. If there is a burn ban on, you will have to skip the bonfire and be extra cautious with candles. Mother Nature would *not* approve if you start a forest fire.

Casual or committed?

This is an important issue to discuss at the start of a new coven or if joining an existing one. Different people have differing expectations and desires when it comes to practicing Witchcraft with others, and I have seen more than one group run into problems when some of the members thought they were just hanging out when it was convenient and others believed they were part of a committed group.

You want to make sure that everyone is on the same page or there will be disappointment, resentment, and possibly an ugly falling-out in your future.

This doesn't mean that you can't start out casual and become more committed (my first group eventually did that after a number of years of people coming and going)—or even do it the other way around. It simply means that whether you have two people or ten, they should all agree on what is expected from coven members and the general approach to practicing magic together.

As I mentioned earlier, Blue Moon Circle always had a small, committed core, although for many years we were open to being joined for rituals by other witches we knew. However, those tended to be a rotating bunch of regulars, not random strangers, and we didn't allow anyone outside the main members to bring along a guest without running it by me first.

Essentially there are two different kinds of covens: open and closed. An open coven is willing to have outsiders attend, and a closed coven is only for those who are members. Obviously, there is some middle ground. Blue Moon Circle is a closed coven, but we occasionally invite friends to join us, and if there is someone we think might be a good fit for the group, we might have them attend a few times as a guest before inviting them to join on a permanent basis.

Open covens may not be a committed group (which doesn't mean that the people who take part aren't committed to their Witchcraft practice, just that there is no expectation that they will all attend on a regular basis). Closed covens usually are committed, but that doesn't mean that they can't be casual in some of the ways they approach Witchcraft.

For instance, during 2020, the first year of COVID-19, Blue Moon Circle only managed to get together a few times—for the summer solstice and the autumn equinox, when it was warm enough to be outside, wearing masks and distancing. Normally we would have done some kind of ritual, but none of us were in the right headspace for deep spiritual work, so we agreed to simply gather and have a feast around the fire pit. At that point, being together was enough of a celebration of our magical bond.

So whether you decide to be a casual group or a more committed one, keep in mind that it is okay to be flexible in your practice as long as everyone involved agrees. Later in the book I talk in more depth about some of the variations on types of group practice.

Who leads?

In traditional Wiccan covens, there was almost always a high priest and a high priestess who led the group, often after having gone through three levels of training under other high priests and high priestesses and then "hiving off" into leading their own coven. These days, you may still find some groups that are led this way, but there are also a lot more options that move beyond this model.

I am in no way denigrating Wicca. I started out in an offshoot of Wicca, and much of how I practice clearly comes from those roots. Modern Witchcraft wouldn't exist on the level it does without all the Wiccan leaders who brought it back into the public eye. I'm just saying that while it works for some, it isn't for everyone, and there are plenty of alternative ways to practice Witchcraft. As you will hear me repeat many times in this and all my other books, there is no one right way, only the way that is right for you.

The group where I spent my first six years as a witch was led by a high priestess who had gotten her training in a traditional Wiccan coven. When we did formal public rituals, she usually had one of the men in the coven act as high priest, but that was only for the duration of the ritual itself. Otherwise we just had her as high priestess.

There have never been any male members of Blue Moon Circle, although we have had the occasional husband or male friend as a guest, so we were always led by a high priestess—me. These days we're a lot more eclectic in our practice, and I don't even use the title anymore, even though I'm almost always the one writing and leading the ritual.

This was a personal choice, brought about in part because I feel that after all this time, we are all equals, every one of us a priestess in her own right, and therefore the "high" part of that term seemed wrong. Also, honestly, it just doesn't matter to us. Some covens have high priests or high priestesses; ours doesn't.

In some cases, like my friend Lisa and the friend she shares her magical work with, there simply aren't enough people involved to bother with the concept of leadership. In other cases, when the practice is more free-flowing and spontaneous, whoever feels like coming up with the ritual and organizing that particular meeting will probably lead. In the case of groups like that, leadership is a temporary role, not a permanent one.

For some covens, this won't be a matter for discussion. If, for instance, the group is founded by one or two people, they may automatically assume the role of leader. In many covens, including mine, no one else wants the job! If you are joining a preexisting coven, this aspect will no doubt already be firmly in place before you get there.

If you are starting a new coven and inviting individuals to join, you will want to consider if this is a role you want permanently or if you just want to get things going and then let people take turns. If a group of people has come together with the goal of starting a coven, you're definitely going to want to discuss the "who leads" question early on so there are no misunderstandings.

Keep in mind that there is no right or wrong way to do this. Many modern eclectic witches may not be comfortable with the terms "high priest" and "high priestess" or want to use gender-specific titles at all. You can always just say "coven leader" or "facilitator" or any other word you all agree upon. Or you may decide you don't need a leader, per se, and just agree on various roles: one person writes the ritual, another organizes the feast, a third cleans and prepares the space. Just because these jobs are traditionally done by whoever leads the coven doesn't mean it has to be that way. These days, every coven is different.

Who is welcome?

One thing you may not consider when starting a new coven is what kind of members you want to include. In the excitement of embarking on a new spiritual adventure, it is easy to think *We want everyone!* I know I did.

Having been part of a large-ish, ever-expanding group, when I set out to create Blue Moon Circle (the name actually came later), I had it in my head that this was what I was aiming for: a varied bunch, as many like-minded people as I could find, ALL THE WITCHES.

As it turned out, the founding members of the group were three in number. Two women I knew slightly, both of whom had practiced as solitaries for years because they'd never found a coven that suited them, and me. For the first year or two, although we invited plenty of friends to the sabbat rituals, full moons and new moons were just the three of us. In fact, we were such a small group that if one of us couldn't make it, we would often cancel. So initially, we only met once in a blue moon. (Get it?)

At first I was disappointed because I had been so certain I wanted a larger coven. But over time, I came to realize that smaller was actually a better fit for both my personality and the way I practice magic. Small groups can be much more intimate, and sometimes it is easier to focus when you have fewer people, especially if your larger group contains folks who aren't as serious about their craft or have a tendency to get distracted and chatter mid-ritual.

Over the years, we have had as many as eleven members and have gone back down to five, one of whom lives farther away now and has a crazy busy life so she can only make it a few times a year. And it turns out that we like being smaller better, so you never know.

We also turned out to be a women-only coven. That wasn't part of the plan either. Initially, we simply didn't find any men who were interested in joining. (We live in a small area where there seem to be fewer male witches, although the larger town to our south has plenty, and their covens seem about evenly split.) Our sabbat rituals often include the Pagan-friendly husband of one of our members and the occasional other male guest, but the group itself never ended up having men in it. Over the years, we've come to the conclusion that we like it that way. Not because we don't like men but because it allows us to have a level of freedom to express ourselves as women that we don't often get in the other facets of our lives.

You can see that some aspects of the "who do we want in our coven" question may not be answered until you have been practicing together for a while. Time and experience may tell you things you didn't know in the beginning. Circumstances will also play a role since you can't always control who will and won't be interested in joining.

And, of course, some covens won't care. There are groups, especially the larger ones, that are open to all, in which case this won't be an issue. If, however, you are starting out as a closed or semi-closed coven, you should probably discuss what kind of members you are willing to include. Consider the following:

Level of experience. Some witches are just starting out and know very little about the actual practice of the Craft. They may have gotten all their knowledge from books and never taken part in an actual live ritual or have been practicing a bit on their own but not for very long. There's nothing wrong with that, and in some cases a coven may be made up of all beginners who learn together.

There are also witches who have been practicing for many years and may be looking for a deeper, more intense experience. A coven may choose to include members of various levels of experience or decide they prefer to only focus on whichever stage the initial founding witches are at when they start out their practice together.

Age. Many covens are made up of people of various ages from eighteen to eighty. Others tend to attract those of a similar age, especially if they are formed from a group of friends. My daughter Jenn's casual group is made up of her peers, so they are mostly all in their thirties, give or take a few years.

I started Blue Moon Circle when I was forty-four, and our core members ranged from late twenties to fifty. Age was less of a factor than the fact that we were all fairly settled in our lives, working serious jobs and involved in serious relationships (if we were in one at all).

Some covens allow teens and others don't. This can be a tricky area, and you may wish to get a parent's permission before including a teen who isn't attending with one of their parents. Either way, the important question is whether or not the members are comfortable being with those who are far outside their age group and whether you all want the same things out of a magical practice.

Age may or may not be a factor in this. At one point two enthusiastic young college-aged women joined our group. They were very much newbies when it came to Witchcraft, but they were also at such a different place in their lives than the rest of us that it made it hard for them to mesh with the rest of the group. On the other hand, the fourteen-year-old daughter of one of our members, who has been coming for her entire life, seems to do just fine when she attends sabbat rituals. So you never know.

No kids allowed? When we're talking about age, it is worth addressing the issue of having children at your rituals. This is less a matter of who is part of your coven, since it is unlikely you would ever consider a child to be a member, and more a matter of whether or not your group is comfortable having children in a ritual setting. My original coven didn't allow kids except the occasional teen, but we were sometimes guests of another group that did, allowing the children to run wild and cause distractions.

The larger semi-public rituals I attended in a nearby town often ran for an entire weekend, with families camping on the land where the rituals were held. It could be a little chaotic, but most folks were pretty good about keeping their kids under control and away from any activities that might be inappropriate (I usually went for Beltane, so you can just imagine what those activities might have been…).

Blue Moon Circle was a true family coven. My daughter, then in her early twenties, attended for a while before she moved away in search of warmer climes. One member had children who didn't attend but always came to our Yule dinner party, which included spouses, kids, and close friends. And then there was Robin. She got married after the coven was started; I officiated, and all the others were there. When she eventually had her two children, they came to rituals—first as babes in the womb, then as breastfeeding babies who were passed around the circle so mom could take a turn doing things, and then as young children being raised as Pagans (along with their father's Christian heritage).

Once they were a bit older and could be left home with their dad, we reclaimed full moons for the adults, but they still came to most sabbat rituals. I happily adjusted the ritual to include them in ways that worked, and with two parents present, there was always someone to supervise each child and, if necessary, remove them from the circle if they started acting up. Robin's son eventually lost interest in the whole thing, but her teen daughter still comes a few times a year and seems to get a lot out of being a part of our circle.

Mind you, as we've all gotten older, we are pretty happy *not* to have small children in attendance, so this is really a matter of individual comfort levels. Some covens are definitely adult-only, and some are family friendly. You just want to be clear about which one you are, especially if you are being joined by a new member who has small children or you have invited a guest who might make an assumption that it is fine to bring their kids along unless you tell them otherwise.

To teach or not to teach?

The first group I belonged to was very much a teaching coven—to the extent that in the beginning, our high priestess referred to it as a study group. We just happened to be studying magic. I will always be grateful to her for her willingness to pass on her knowledge, and the six years I spent with that group taught me much of what I know about Witchcraft, including what I do and don't want from a group practice. My life would have been completely different without that teaching, and these books probably wouldn't exist.

But not every coven wants to go that route. It can be difficult to move on with a magical practice if you continually have to go back to the beginning to instruct those new to the Craft. Blue Moon Circle originally was open to any level, but after having those younger women with no experience join us for a while, we decided that we really didn't want to be a teaching coven. They were lovely, but once they moved on, we had a discussion and agreed that we wanted to be able to focus on deeper work.

But that was us, and you may have a completely different take on things. Some people get as much joy from sharing their knowledge as they do from learning. Others consider it an obligation to the next generation of witches. For me, I prefer to teach through my writing and by answering individual questions from those who contact me, but every community can benefit from a coven that is willing to teach.

Who will we worship?

Witchcraft is a nature-based religion that encompasses a wide range of belief systems. Most witches worship both the God and the Goddess, although a few only follow the Goddess. Some call on specific deities while others take a more general approach; some may simply refer to the universe. None of this matters when a witch is solitary, but when multiple Pagans come together in a group, you may need to make some compromises to make sure that everyone involved is comfortable with the way the group relates to and refers to deity. In Blue Moon Circle's practice, we usually call on both the God and the Goddess during sabbat rituals, sometimes in a general "we invoke the God and Goddess" format and sometimes invoking specific deities who are associated with that particular sabbat, such as Brigid at Imbolc.

On full moons we only call on the Goddess or specific goddesses. We are primarily Goddess-oriented and have enjoyed exploring the aspects of various goddesses to expand our knowledge beyond those who we might call on when practicing on our own. This will vary from coven to coven and possibly from ritual to ritual if you take turns leading. Just be careful to be aware of and respect the individual approaches and desires of those involved, if necessary finding some middle ground.

When It Isn't Working

—dealing with issues—

Having been a part of two different covens and seeing what has happened in numerous others, I can tell you with some certainty that if you practice together with more than one other person (and possibly even then), you will eventually have issues. They may be minor or they may be large enough to cause the coven to disband, but either way, you should be prepared to deal with them when they come up.

My best advice to you here is to make sure that you have open communication within your group and that everyone feels free to speak up if something is bothering them. Even Blue Moon Circle has had occasional bumps in the road over our long years practicing together, and every single time they could have been prevented by better communication. Thankfully, we've gotten better at this over time.

If you are leading a coven, be sure that you are open to suggestions and concerns, and try to pay attention to hints that any of your members might be unhappy. Many times people don't feel comfortable speaking up, but if you ask, "Hey, is something bothering you?" you might discover they have been sitting on an issue you could have resolved long ago if only you'd known about it. Yes, this *is* the voice of experience.

If you are part of a coven, remember that no one can fix a problem if they don't know what it is. If you are unhappy about something—whether it is how the coven is being run, aspects of the ritual practice, or the fact that Sue always brings that horrible tuna casserole to every feast—you need to be open about the issue and allow your fellow coven members to search for a solution that works for everyone.

If you can't trust them to accept your input, as long as you are nice about it, you are probably in the wrong coven. Interpersonal problems are probably the biggest cause of covens imploding and falling apart. I have known of covens that were led by a couple, and when the couple split, some members went with one person and the rest with the other. I've also seen a situation where a high priestess got a new boyfriend and brought him into the coven. When he didn't get along with several members, they were tossed out to keep him happy.

Nobody said witches were perfect. We're all human beings. If there are members of the coven who don't get along, you can try discussing why that is. Sometimes someone simply isn't a good fit for a group or causes problems with everyone, in which case it is up to the group leader to ask them to leave. This is always a tough situation, although in my experience, most of the time these people aren't happy in the coven either and simply stop attending. But this is one of the reasons why it pays to be cautious about adding new members if you don't know them well, and making sure you establish clear communication from the very beginning.

General Rules for Any Group

For the most part, Witchcraft as a spiritual path doesn't have nearly as many rules as most other religions. We're not all that big on the "shalt nots," as it were, and even the most basic of rules, such as "harm none," isn't agreed on by everyone. That being said, there are a few general rules that you should expect to follow if you are part of a coven. Plus, of course, any rules that your group in particular agrees on in addition to these. (Some covens, for instance, are very strict about not speaking about the coven to outsiders. Others aren't.)

If you are new to practicing magic together or if you add new people to your coven, it is probably a good idea to make sure that everyone involved understands these few basic guidelines:

- **Everyone in the group should be treated with respect and kindness.** You wouldn't think this needs to be spelled out, but sometimes that's necessary. It is said that we enter the ritual circle "in perfect love and perfect trust." This doesn't mean you have to love everyone in your coven, but you have to at least like them and be willing to accept them with an open heart, no matter their imperfections, at least during the time you are sharing ritual or a group practice. Criticism and judgmental comments have no place in circle.

- **What is said in circle stays in circle.** This is where the trust part comes in. People often speak about very private things when they are in sacred space. The members of your coven need to know that anything they say within the confines of group practice, both in and out of the ritual circle, will be held in strict confidence.

- **Never "out" someone as a witch if you aren't certain this is common knowledge.** As the published author of many books on Witchcraft, I am obviously firmly out of the broom closet. Anyone who doesn't know that I'm a witch simply hasn't been paying attention. But that isn't true for everyone. Over the years, Blue Moon Circle has included a number of people who weren't free to be public about their spiritual path because of their jobs (including a nurse, a library professional who worked with children, and a teacher). There were others who simply felt it was no one else's business and didn't choose to tell anyone other than those closest to them. It can be easy to forget this and greet someone in your coven with a hearty "Merry meet!" or ask if they are coming to this month's sabbat ritual when there are others within earshot. Take care to protect your group members' privacy unless you are told otherwise.
- **Accept the people in your coven as who they are and respect their personal choices and preferences.** This is more important now than ever, as our society struggles with equality and acceptance on a much larger scale. There are many who come to Witchcraft because they feel they cannot be accepted by religion or culture they were raised within. LGBTQ+ people in particular have found a home in the Pagan community. People of color sometimes still struggle to do so. If someone in your group asks to be addressed as "they" instead of "he" or "she," do your best to respect their wishes. If someone does not act or dress in a

conventional manner, embrace and honor that. After all, you want to be accepted as who you are, don't you? If we can't do that in sacred space, we can't do it anywhere.

• • •

When you come together with other witches in a group, large or small, and everything clicks, it can be an incredibly rewarding experience. There is great joy in sharing your spiritual path with like-minded people, and amazing power can be raised when a bunch of witches work together toward a common goal.

For many of us, our covens become the family we chose rather than the family we were born into, and the bonds that are formed within a shared magical practice are like no other.

It is worth the effort it takes to make a group practice work for all those involved, and the rewards you reap are more than equal to the investment of time, energy, and heart that you put into it.

A Note about Supplies

In the rituals that follow, as well as any you may come up with on your own, there will usually be some kind of supplies. These often include candles, herbs, stones, and various miscellaneous other ingredients for spells and crafts. Some of these may be things that participants can contribute from their gardens or personal stocks. Others will have to be purchased. Over the course of time, this can get expensive, although not onerously so if you choose to keep things fairly basic. In some covens, the leader or leaders provide the supplies. I tend to do this because I can get them wholesale; also I tend to have a bunch of candles and stones around anyway.

In my first group, the high priestess eventually asked people to contribute to a "supply jar" in whatever amount they felt they could comfortably manage. In other groups, people either chip in, take turns providing supplies, or each person brings their own if they are told ahead of time what is needed. How your coven chooses to handle this will depend in part on the finances of those involved and also in how the group is run. But this is another area where expectations should be made clear from the outset, especially to new members, and everyone should agree on the approach so no one feels too big a burden.

Section 2

Ritual Basics

Like everything else in a Witchcraft practice, rituals are open to personal interpretation and individual preferences. When you are working with a coven, however, it is a good idea to agree on the basics so that you are all doing the same steps to the same dance, so to speak.

Rituals can be as simple as lighting a candle and saying a spell or so complicated they take an hour to complete. There are benefits to both approaches. If time is short or the people taking part aren't inclined toward long, involved magical workings, you can definitely lean toward the simple side of things. If the work is serious and needs all the power it can get or if your group enjoys the pageantry and beauty of a deeper, more layered rite, then by all means go for the entire traditional ritual.

Or do something in between. Maybe you want to keep things basic on the full moons and get more complicated for the sabbats. Maybe you'll change things up depending on the moods and energy levels of those in your coven. Perhaps you'll feel that some occasions (such as Samhain, which can be an intense holiday for many) merit pulling out all the stops, and that others (like Yule, which may be more celebratory) can be done in a more relaxed fashion.

Blue Moon Circle usually follows a formal ritual format, from cleansing and casting the circle to calling the quarters, invoking the Goddess and God, doing the main part of whatever the magical working is, then sharing cakes and ale before dismissing the circle. But there have been times, especially lately, when we opt to take a more casual approach. Then we usually start by passing the purifying herbs, which always brings us into the right spiritual mental space, and then launch straight into whatever it is we're doing.

Of course, part of the reason we can do this is that we have been practicing together for such a long time, we have a well-established rhythm and come together as one without much effort. If you're newer to working together as a group or if there are a large amount of people involved (or people who are new to your group), you may find it helpful to go through all the steps of a more ceremonial approach. This will serve to pull you together into a more cohesive whole and move you all deeper into a more focused and grounded state, which in turn will make your magical work more powerful.

Keep in mind that you can follow some of these steps and leave out the ones that don't appeal to you. You can also choose to have one person lead the entire ritual or have different individuals take on specific roles. For instance, the group leader (such as a high priest or high priestess, if you have one, or whoever happened to write that day's ritual) may cast the circle, call the quarters, invoke the gods, and lead the magical part of the ritual. Or you could have different coven members who are responsible for certain sections, either for one particular ritual or every time you meet.

I almost always lead our rituals, although we take turns going around the circle and having people call the quarter closest to where they are standing or sometimes use an invocation that has us calling the quarters and invoking the Goddess in unison. At the end the quarters are dismissed by those who called them. We also usually open and close the circle together. In addition, periodically one of the other coven members will take a turn at leading a ritual, which gives me a chance to just relax and enjoy taking part instead of doing all the work.

If you are just starting out, you may want to experiment with various approaches to see what works best for you as a group. Don't worry if things don't go smoothly every time—or even any time. We often end up forgetting something, messing up when we call quarters, or things just generally don't go the way we had intended. We are infamous for our inability to light the sage wand, candles, or the bonfire, to the point where we joke about being fire-impaired witches. We just laugh and keep going. Modern witches often say they practice magic with reverence and mirth, and Blue Moon Circle definitely enjoys having a bit of both.

The General Framework of Ritual Work

These are the basic parts of ritual that are used by many modern witches and Pagans. Very traditional Wiccan covens may have additional steps, and more eclectic groups sometimes come up with their own individual spin on things. Witchcraft is an evolving and changing spiritual path, and your practice may end up looking very different from someone else's.

As always, there is no wrong way to do this. Pick and choose from the options I've listed here or invent your own way of doing things. As long as you create an environment in which all those who are taking part feel comfortable and can hone their focus to raise energy for the magical work you are doing and feel the power of spirit that lies within a sacred circle, it really doesn't matter how you go about getting there. Just remember reverence and mirth, and you'll be fine.

Under most circumstances, the group leader (or leaders), with or without the help of others, will set up the circle with whatever items are needed for the magical work you will be doing (quarter and deity candles, an altar, whatever you are using for that specific ritual, etc.) before the rest of these steps are done, so that everything is ready to go as soon as the coven is assembled.

Preparing the circle space. This may be something the ritual leader or a group member does before the ritual even begins. To prepare the space for the more magical energy of the ritual, some use a broom or besom (one kept only for magical work) to sweep away any negative energy or clear the space's mundane energy, especially if it is an area like a living room that is normally used in regular life.

This can also be done with purifying herbs, incense, salt and water, or even a large feather or a bell. What matters is that it is done with focus and intent, not so much what you use. If a space is only used for magical work, like the ritual circle behind my barn, this eventually becomes unnecessary, although it certainly won't hurt. On the other hand, some groups never do this step. The only time I would consider it truly necessary would be if you are using a shared space (say, one at a public building that is used by other groups of people for various activities) or one that has some unpleasant lingering energy (for instance, a living room in the house of a couple who fights a lot). Otherwise, this is optional or can be done as part of the cleansing and consecrating step listed below.

Entering the circle. This can be a very formal step of the ritual (where people form a line and process into the circle space) or very informal (where folks simply mill around and find a spot to stand). Larger rituals, especially those held outside, may tend to use the first approach.

We did that for many years for our sabbat rituals when we might have as many as twelve to fifteen people attending, including guests. My outdoor circle is behind my barn/garage and is reached by walking up a short sloping path. When we had nighttime rituals, we would put tall oil-fueled torches at the bottom and top of the path to make it even more magical. For truly formal events, we would have one of the members standing up at the top to greet people with a phrase such as "Welcome to our circle; enter in perfect love and perfect trust" and anoint their foreheads with a magical oil.

The benefit of the more ceremonial approach is that it puts people into the ritual mindset right away and reminds them that they are entering sacred space. This can be important if you are working with a large group, especially if some of them are strangers. In some cases, I also suggest doing a quick run-through of the rules of circle etiquette or handing out a sheet with the information you'll find later in the book. Never assume everyone knows the do's and don'ts of proper ritual behavior.

On the other hand, if you only have a few people or if everyone in your coven practices together on a regular basis, you may find that just saying "Okay, let's get started now" is enough to gather everyone together in a quiet and ready manner.

Cleansing and consecrating the space. Unlike most religions, where there is a specific building that is a permanent structure designated for use as a spiritual space, such as a church or a temple or a mosque, witches rarely have that luxury—or really even the need for it. We can create sacred space wherever we want it simply by casting a magical circle. Some covens actually have longstanding circles, like the traditional nine-foot stone ring embedded in the ground behind the barn at my house, but much of the time sacred space is created for the duration of the ritual, then dismissed when you are done using it.

Either way, at the start of a ritual it is common practice to cleanse and consecrate the circle area for magical use, thus turning it into sacred space. We often cleanse ourselves at the same time. These actions turn the circle into a safe place for working powerful magic and also serve to ground and center those taking part, reminding them that they are leaving the mundane world behind so they can focus on the magical work ahead.

You can do as few or as many of these options as you choose, but keep in mind that if you use the same general structure for most rituals, over time it will become a subliminal cue to those taking part and help them move more easily into the ritual frame of mind. For Blue Moon Circle, passing purifying herbs has become a signal that we are leaving the mundane world behind, and we all seem to take a deep breath without even intending to and become that much more present in sacred space.

Try a few of these and see which ones work the best for your coven, and then integrate them into your magical work on a regular basis. If you are doing a number of different things, you can have members of your group take turns doing one rather than having the leader (if you have one) do them all. Most of the time these should be done in reverence and silence to aid in deepening the feeling of entering a spiritual realm.

- Sweep around the outside of the circle with a broom kept for magical work.
- Walk around the outside of the circle space with purifying herbs or incense.
- Pass purifying herbs or incense from person to person within the circle. The smoke should be wafted from head to toe (or the reverse) to cleanse the body of any negativity brought in from the outside world.
- Pass a dish of salt mixed with water and have those taking part anoint themselves (usually at brow, lips, heart, and center of the belly); sometimes the high priestess or group leader blesses the water and salt mixture first, imbuing it with the intention of washing away anything negative or unhelpful.
- A group member can walk around the outside of the circle sprinkling salt and water or first salt and then water separately.
- Ring a bell or strike a gong or a drum to signal the formal start of ritual.

Cast the circle. Everything you have done so far has led up to this moment. This is when you formally state your intent to create a magical and sacred space. In traditional Wicca, the high priest or priestess often walks around the outside of the circle with an athame or a magical sword. I used to do this back in the beginning of our practice, saying something like: "I cast the circle round and round, from earth to sky, from sky to ground. I conjure now this sacred space, outside time and outside space. The circle is cast, we are between the worlds."

These days we are more casual and usually cast the circle "from hand to hand," which means I take the hand of the person to my left (movement inside a ritual circle is always clockwise (deosil), unless you are doing some kind of unbinding or release) and say: "We cast the circle hand to hand." When we are all attached, I then say: "The circle is cast; we are in sacred space between the worlds"—or words to that effect.

You can also cast the circle by passing an object, like a flower during a summer solstice ritual or a bell that each person rings in turn. Or simply have everyone say in turn: "The circle is cast." Whichever way you choose to do it, if done with focus and intent, you will actually feel the atmosphere inside the circle change. The air is not quite the same. You may feel more power or potential. Even two people can achieve this if they are working in harmony.

Keep in mind that once you have cast the circle, people are no longer free to just wander in and out. If someone wishes to cross into or out of sacred space, it is traditional to cut a "doorway" by having another person trace the shape of a door with their finger or an athame. Otherwise you run the risk of simply bursting the bubble you put all that energy into creating.

Call the quarters. Once the circle is cast, the next step is usually to invoke the four quarters, calling in the elements of earth, air, fire, and water to guard the circle and lend their strength to those inside it. It is also a way to connect us to the elements, which are an important part of a Witchcraft practice. The quarters, traditionally referred to as watchtowers, are laid out with earth in the north, then air to the east, fire to the south, and finally water to the west, and each is usually represented by a candle in a specific color (green or brown, yellow, red, and blue, respectively).

The candles may be placed at the outer edges of the circle or on an altar in the middle or you can do without them altogether if you are in a place where you can't have anything burning (a dorm, for instance, or a convention held in a hotel). If you prefer, you can use all white candles.

Some people substitute items that represent the elements, such as a feather or incense for air. In Blue Moon Circle, we usually have different people call the quarters and light the candles that are closest to where they are standing. Most people start with the east, but some folks start with north instead. It is usual for everyone in the circle to turn and face the direction being called, and some people lift a finger or an athame to point toward that quarter (this is a traditional Wiccan approach), but you certainly don't have to.

For more formal rituals, we may use words that have been written out ahead on slips of paper—this can be more comfortable for people as they are starting out and don't feel confident in knowing what to say or on occasions when you want to use more flowery or specific language for a particular sabbat—but most of the time we just speak whatever words come to us. It doesn't have to be anything more complicated than the basics: "I call the east, the power of air, to come and guard our circle," although it can also be much more detailed. There are examples later in the book.

We also have a beautiful combined quarter call and invocation to the Goddess that one of our members found online years ago. This is intended to be recited in unison, with everyone turning to face in the direction being called at that moment and then turning back to the center to invoke the Goddess. We have found it to be very powerful and moving, especially at the full moon, as we speak with one voice. I should note that some people also call in the powers below and above, calling on the energy of the ground and the sky.

Invoke the Goddess and the God. Or just the Goddess, depending on how you practice or what the occasion is. There are some witches who only call on the Goddess, and if that is your preference, that's fine. Blue Moon Circle invokes both the God and the Goddess on the sabbats, but only the Goddess when we celebrate the full moon.

You can call on specific deities—for instance, ones who are associated with a particular holiday or time of year, or ones who you feel can best assist you with whatever magical work you will be doing. Or you can simply say something general, like "We invoke the Goddess and ask her to join us in our magical circle." As with calling the quarters, a candle is usually lit when doing an invocation.

For the Goddess, people often use silver or white, and for the God, gold or cream or yellow. Sometimes particular deities have a color associated with them. Remember to be respectful; you are asking for a deity to honor you with their presence, after all. Some people have a patron god or goddess and call on that deity in particular whenever they do magic, but in a group that is less likely to happen, unless you all follow Diana, for instance.

Welcome and introduction. This probably won't be something you do if you are working with a very small coven, but for larger groups or times when you have guests, whoever is leading the ritual usually greets the participants and explains a little bit about the occasion ("We're here to celebrate Samhain, one of the most sacred days on the Pagan calendar") and what you will be doing during the ritual ("Tonight we will drum and dance to raise energy, write our wishes for the new year on pieces of paper that we will stick inside this corn dolly, and then throw it into the bonfire as we say a spell together"). This is a helpful way to get everyone into the ritual mood while also letting participants know what to expect.

If there are just two or three of you, it is fine to skip this part, especially if you are a less formal group, although Blue Moon Circle still does this sometimes even when there are only four of us. I knew a group leader who called this part the "ritual rap," which kind of cracked me up.

Magical working. This is the main part of the ritual, and it can consist of one or more aspects of magical and spiritual practice. Some of the more common approaches include guided meditation (usually but not always led by whoever is in charge of the ritual), trancework, drumming, chanting, dancing, lighting a bonfire, doing something crafty with magical intentions (such as sewing a poppet, creating a vision board, making healing herbal sachets, etc.), divination, and, of course, spellwork.

Some components done during this point in the ritual may be used to draw the participants deeper into a focused mental state, some are used to build energy that will then be channeled into the magical work, and some are just plain fun. The options are endless, and you can practice for years and never do exactly the same ritual twice.

What you choose to do for any given ritual will depend on the occasion, the way your coven prefers to practice (Blue Moon Circle is made up of a bunch of crafty women, so we often do some sort of craft project), the time and energy people have to devote to that particular ritual, and any specific needs of those involved in the group.

For instance, you may choose to do a healing ritual if one or more of your coven members are having health issues or prosperity work if you could all use a financial boost. We almost always do something to raise energy and then end by channeling it into a spell. But you don't have to have a particular goal in mind, and sometimes it is nice to get together simply in celebration.

Grounding. If a ritual is particularly intense, it can leave you feeling buzzy and a little disconnected. One way to avoid that is to ground some of the extra energy you've just generated back into the earth by putting your hands flat on the ground and consciously channeling it away from you. Alternately, you can send it down through your feet, although I find that the first approach works better for me.

Cakes and ale. We particularly enjoy this part of the ritual, although it isn't strictly necessary. Once the magical work is done, cakes (which can be cookies, bread, or even seasonal fruit) and ale (which is usually either wine, mead, or juice, especially if there are kids present) are passed around the circle.

The sharing of food and drink is traditional and celebrates the gifts the gods have given us, but it also serves to ground you back in the real world and reconnect you with your physical body. The group leader may bless the cakes and ale before sending them around the circle, and we often say "May you never hunger" and "May you never thirst" or "May you always have enough to eat and someone to share it with" (or words to that effect) to each other as we hand off the plate or goblet.

If you are doing ritual outside, you may wish to pour out a libation to the gods onto the ground or leave a bit of food for the faeries and other elementals, or even for the creatures of the earth who live on the land.

Pass the speaking stick. Not everyone does this, and we don't do it every time, but it is a nice way to wind down a ritual. The speaking stick is symbolic, and it can be an actual stick or a stone, a feather, or a group staff if you happen to have one. The item is passed around the circle and each person gets a chance to speak from the heart. This may be as simple as saying thank you for the ritual and how glad they are to be there or it might be something raw and personal that was brought up during ritual.

The most important thing to remember is that only the person holding the stick should be talking; everyone else should be focusing their complete attention on what that person is saying. This can be difficult in larger groups, especially when you get someone who rambles on (and you will), but for some people, this may literally be the only time in their lives when they are free to say exactly what they are thinking or feeling. It can be very cathartic.

If at all possible, listen with an open heart and without judging. If you do have someone who doesn't know when to stop talking, it may be necessary for whoever is leading the ritual to gently suggest that the stick be passed to the next person, but luckily this doesn't happen often. The leader or someone who is close to that person may choose to wait until after the ritual is over and speak to the person in private to not risk embarrassing them.

Dismiss the quarters. This is the reverse of when you called in the quarters at the start of the ritual, so if you started with east and ended with north, to dismiss the quarters you would start in the north and move counterclockwise (widdershins) around the circle, with the same people dismissing a quarter who called it in when you began.

The candles are blown or snuffed out one by one. (Traditional Wiccans are taught that it is disrespectful to blow the flames out and that they should be snuffed out instead. To be honest, I've never understood this one, and we usually blow them out. It's up to you.) Dismissals can be as simple as, "Power of air, we thank you for watching over our circle and lending us your energy. Blessed be." Or if the original quarter call was more elaborate, the dismissal might be as well.

Thanking the Goddess and the God. Obviously, one doesn't dismiss a deity; that would be rude. Simply give heartfelt thanks for their presence in your circle and for any help they may have given you. Like everything else, this can be as formal or as casual as you like, as long as it is respectful. Some people say, "Stay if you will, go if you must; in perfect love and perfect trust, so mote it be."

Opening the circle. You can do this in the reverse of however you closed the circle; for instance, if the group leader walked around the outside of the circle with an athame, they would do the same but counterclockwise instead. If you cast the circle hand to hand, you might all join hands again and then let them go. Sometimes this is accompanied by raising hands in the air and letting out a joyful shout.

In its earlier years, Blue Moon Circle often ended by reciting a shorter version of a work known as the Wiccan Rede because that was what my first group used to do. It is traditional for Wiccans, and we enjoyed reciting it in unison. This is the version we used:

Bide the Wiccan law we must
In perfect love and perfect trust.
Eight words the Wiccan Rede fulfill
An' it harm none, do as you will.
Lest in thy self-defense it be
Ever mind the law of three.
Follow this with mind and heart
And merry ye meet and merry ye part!

As our practice grew and changed, shifting somewhat away from my Wiccan roots, we stopped using the more flowery and archaic language in favor of the more simplistic

The circle is open but never broken.
Merry meet, merry part, and merry meet again!

This last bit is usually shouted joyfully.

You can also just visualize the magical walls dropping and allowing the world back in again, and say, "The circle is open. Let's feast!"

A Note on Purifying Herbs, Incense, Feast Food, and Other Things

Keep in mind that there are some people who are allergic to artificial scents (present in many scented candles and most incense, unless it is specifically labeled that it has been made using essential oils). I am one of them and can't be in a room where someone is burning regular incense because it triggers my asthma. In a closed room, even sage can bother sensitive people.

Use unscented candles whenever possible, and be aware that you may have to work around members' issues if working with a group. Most people will let you know if they have problems with common Witchcraft tools, but it never hurts to ask if you are starting a new group or someone joins an existing group.

The same thing goes for cakes and ale—if someone has a gluten sensitivity, for instance, you may want to use something for cakes that they can still partake in. And before serving alcohol (such as mead or actual ale) in your chalice, make sure you don't have any attendees who are in recovery or underage.

When it comes to feasts, smaller covens usually know each other well enough to be aware of food issues. But if you have a larger group or an open group that allows guests, make sure you have options that vegetarians can eat, and if you want to go that extra mile, have each person make up a card to put with their feast offering that lists the ingredients. That way people with allergies can avoid anything problematic.

Variations on a Theme

Keep in mind that just because most witches—or some witches or even the witch who wrote this book—do things in a particular way, that doesn't mean you have to follow suit. Everyone has their own path and their own preferences, and as long as the folks in your coven agree on an approach, you can pretty much do as you please. (You know, within reason. Let's try not to set things on fire unintentionally or terrify the neighbors too often.)

Witchcraft is a growing, changing, and evolving practice, and no two witches are guaranteed to believe exactly the same things or practice their craft in exactly the same way. In fact, some people view it as a religion (the fastest growing one in North America, I might point out). For others it is a spiritual path, and the word *religion* may make them uncomfortable. For me, it is a little of both.

Some people aren't comfortable with the word *coven* either and prefer to say *group* or *circle* or not call it anything in particular at all. Some still use a high priestess or a high priest, and some just say *leader*. Others don't even do that, preferring to let people take turns leading instead.

As you can see from the Wiccan Rede, the origins of Wicca were often couched in ornate, archaic styles of speaking. Participants wore formal robes (or sometimes nothing at all) and went through complicated initiations and multiple levels of training. This is less common now, although there are versions of this practice that still exist and this approach is great if it appeals to you.

There are also many specific types of Witchcraft, such as Gardnerian, Alexandrian, Traditional, Feri, Reclaiming, Celtic, or other practices that focus on a particular pantheon of gods. Not to mention kitchen witches (who channel their magical practices through food and cooking) and green witches, hearth witches, and hedge witches. In short, whatever kind of Witchcraft you wish to practice, there is probably one that will suit you.

Some of the more traditional approaches may require you to be initiated and follow specific rules.

Eclectic witches, on the other hand, tend to take a bit of whatever works and meld it together into their own personal style. This is probably the fastest-growing segment of the Witchcraft population, and if you don't identify with any of the other types of witches, you might decide—either personally or as a group—to take this approach. Over our years of practice together, Blue Moon Circle has moved away from the more traditional Wiccan coven and now consider ourselves to be an eclectic coven, although we still use plenty of Wiccan bits and pieces. Really, just do whatever works for you, whatever you choose to call it.

Certainly it is not necessary to be at all formal in your practice if that doesn't appeal to you. We did a group dedication when we first started practicing together but never did individual ones or initiations or levels. We still enjoy some more ceremonial rituals from time to time, but we also have no problem being more casual and laid-back, especially if we're all feeling tired or stressed.

If you are starting a new coven, it is important to discuss as a group whether you want to adhere to traditional Wiccan practices, follow some particular already established path, or create your own. Don't hesitate to try different things and then discuss which elements worked for you and which didn't. If you don't all agree, work on some kind of compromise so everyone gets at least some of what they want at least some of the time and no one ever has to do anything that truly makes them uncomfortable.

If you are joining an existing coven, make sure that their style and beliefs mesh with your own. If something makes you uncomfortable, pay attention to that feeling and find someplace else.

Witchcraft is constantly changing, and that gives us a kind of flexibility that can be hard to find in more rigid, established religions. Just remember, "An' it harm none, do as you will." As long as you're not hurting anyone, you can design a magical practice that will work for you and for anyone else you choose to share the Craft with on a regular basis.

If you don't feel like casting a circle, try having everyone focus on visualizing a bubble of protective energy surrounding you. If you don't want to call the quarters, you can simply place items that are representative of the elements on your altar. Perhaps just take a moment to feel and appreciate the ground under your feet, the air you breathe, the water that nourishes the plants, and the heat of the sun up above.

I know that there are some people who aren't sure if they believe in a Goddess or a God and aren't comfortable calling on them. That's okay too. Make a space that is magical and sacred, and see what—or who—shows up. As long as your mind and your heart are open, I assure you, they will hear you anyway.

Tools of the Trade

There are a number of tools that are traditionally used by witches and have been associated with them throughout the centuries. Others are somewhat more recent additions that came along with Wicca and the practices that followed. If you have been a witch for a while, you probably know all about most if not all of these and may have many of them in your own collection. If you are just starting, don't feel that you need to run out and buy one (or ten) of everything. Unless it is crystals. You definitely need a bunch of those. Or books. You can't have enough books. Sorry, what was I saying? (Yes, every witch has their own obsessions. It kind of comes with the territory.)

And as with everything else, your preferences may change over time. Initially, I used an athame in my magical work. I probably had three or four over the years. These days I am just as likely to use my finger to point and direct energy, and the athames now act as decorative additions to my altar.

If you are in a coven, there may be some tools that belong to the group as a whole that simply live at someone's house when they are not being used. Blue Moon Circle's tools include a bunch of different drums (a few people have their own; otherwise, we use the ones I got for the group's use), a staff we decorated and consecrated together, a goblet that one of our group made when she was working as a potter, and a speaking stick, among other things. When you create a tool together, it takes on a special meaning and becomes even more powerful and treasured because of the energy you put into it.

Here is a list of some of the basic tools your coven may end up using, either separately or together. Some of them are things you will have to buy; others you can make if you are so inclined. Some of Blue Moon Circle's favorite rituals have involved working together to create tools and magical goodies such as charm bags, whether they are individual ones each person takes home to use or those dedicated to the group. If you are of the crafty witch persuasion, there are some fun projects later on in the book.

Keep in mind that any tool can be blessed and consecrated for positive magical work either when it is finished or later on.

Altar—You might not think of an altar as a tool, but some groups find a table that they can decorate with symbols and designs that are meaningful to their coven. In the case of a permanent outdoor circle, use a large rock or slab of wood. For a group that meets at the same place every time, an altar might be a stationary fixture that is left in place with all the usual tools (candles, etc.) laid out for the next ritual. Or it might be a table or shelf that has another purpose most of the time and is transformed by a pretty cloth and whatever ritual supplies you are using into an altar for the duration of your meeting.

Athame—A witch's knife, usually double-edged. It can be made from any material—from metal to wood to stone—and is used to direct energy or to point, not to actually cut anything. These can be extremely basic and simple or ornate and fancy. If you are going to have a group athame, you might want to use wood, which you can etch or burn symbols, names, or the like into, or find a more standard metal one and attach embellishments to it. Traditionally, the athame represented male energy, although these days there is less emphasis on such things.

Besom—A besom is a kind of broom made of more traditional materials like twigs or rough straw for the bottom part and a natural, usually crooked stick for the handle. It is used less for cleansing and more for moving energy, but they can be very cool looking.

Book of Shadows—Knowledge is the greatest tool of all, and a witch's Book of Shadows often contains notes on herbs, crystals, spells, recipes, and more. Each witch's Book of Shadows is different, and not everyone has one, but I highly recommend them if you are so inclined. It is handy to have all your witchy information gathered in one easy-to-check place in case you need to look up what spell you used for prosperity the last time, since it seemed to work so well, or which herbs you used for that protection sachet. Blue Moon Circle has a group Book of Shadows, which contains copies of all the spells and rituals we have done together, as well as photos from our adventures. Traditional Wiccan covens often had an official coven Book of Shadows from which information was shared with members. Some witches use a simple binder, which they may decorate with pictures, symbols, or even dried flowers. Others buy already made blank books with magical images on them or create their own from scratch.

Books—There are many fabulous books on Witchcraft out there, both old and new, covering every magical topic you can think of. My own personal collection takes up four shelves and encompasses books on stones, herbs, gods and goddesses, holidays, various types of magical work, and much more. And that's not even counting the books I actually wrote, which I refer to quite often when I'm in search of a particular spell or piece of information. While it is true that you can look up most things online these days, I prefer the weight of an actual book and the knowledge that comes from people I know are reliable. Plus, they're right there on the shelf whenever I need them. (Also, it is possible I have a small book addiction. What do you expect from an author?) Your coven may wish to have a revolving book collection and share the knowledge amongst yourselves.

Broom—Sadly, I have never been able to get mine to fly, but a magical broom is still a very useful tool. They can be used to remove negative energy or cleanse a circle, as described earlier, or add an element of magic to your housekeeping by mindfully sweeping away what you no longer want along with the dust. Remember a broom that is used as a magical tool should not be used for everyday cleaning, and if at all possible, it should be made of natural materials (a wooden handle and actual broom straw bristles, rather than plastic). Magical brooms can be hung over entrance doorways to a house to protect it, and people sometimes still follow the old tradition of "jumping the broom" to celebrate a marriage or handfasting.

fun fact: The broom is the only magical tool that represents both the male and the female, with the handle standing for the male energy and the bristles standing for the female.

Cauldron—A deep metal bowl or container often made of cast iron. They usually have three legs, and some of them have a handle that can be used to suspend them over a fire. In the old days, people used them to cook with and they were probably more likely to hold stew than a potion. The image of a witch stirring her cauldron has persisted through the centuries, so there is a strong connection to Witchcraft even today. They come in a variety of sizes, from tiny to huge. I have a small one (about 3 inches across) that is perfect for holding a burning herbal cleansing stick, and a larger one (about a foot across and heavy as hell) that we would fill with sand and use to hold multiple candles for times when we wanted each person taking part to be able to light a number of them. The cauldron represents the Goddess, the womb, and the feminine.

Chalice—A cup or goblet used during ritual, often to hold the "ale" part of cakes and ale but also sometimes used for water or some kind of liquid offering such as mead. While you could use anything for this, most witches have a goblet that is set aside for magical use and not everyday drinking. They can be made of anything from pottery to glass to metal and vary from the simple to the extremely ornate. The one Blue Moon Circle uses was made by one of our members out of clay, which we decorated together, each of us adding our own symbols, and then she covered it with a clear glaze and fired it in a kiln. It lives on an altar at my house, a constant symbol of our unity. When doing coven work, the chalice is often passed around the circle, so it is good to have something that is sturdy as well as pretty. Like the cauldron, the chalice represents the female.

Crystals and stones—As a self-professed stone junkie, I have to confess that I have a lot of crystals. **A LOT**. I use them for magical work and energy healing, and also they're pretty and shiny and make me happy so I just have them all over my house. But that doesn't mean you have to go out and buy All the Stones. Some witches have one or two that they use for most of their magical work, usually a clear quartz crystal (which represents the Goddess and the moon and is an all-around powerful stone) or something like amethyst, which also can be used in many applications. There are plenty of semiprecious stones that aren't terribly expensive, and you can use small tumbled versions instead of large fancy crystals if you choose. Different stones are associated with different attributes—such as rose quartz for love, friendship, and calm—so many witches like to have at least a small collection to use for various magical goals. They are used for focus and to increase power for the work at hand.

Drums, rattles, flutes, bells, and other musical instruments—Music and rhythmic sounds can be powerful magical tools. There is a reason why indigenous people from all around the world use some form of musical instrument in their rituals and spiritual practices. Music can create a mood, draw you into a trance state, or lift your spirits to the point of ecstasy. Clapping, stomping your feet, and dancing are also intrinsic to many spiritual practices. The voice is also a musical instrument, and chanting or singing are often used in magic as well. You don't need to worry about sounding pitch perfect; it's about emotion and intent, not a talent contest. In Blue Moon Circle we use drums the most, but we also have rattles for people who aren't comfortable with drums (not everyone has a natural sense of rhythm). We also do some chanting. In our rituals these things are primarily used to raise energy, which is then channeled into whatever spell we are doing.

Garb—*Garb* is a word for clothing that is used specifically for dressing up. For instance, some folks have Renaissance faire garb that they use when they are attending that type of event. In Witchcraft, the term *garb* is used for clothes that are intended for ritual use or occasionally to attend a witchy convention or gathering.

This may be as simple as a cloak or loose robe that is thrown on over whatever other clothes you are wearing, or it can be an entire outfit that is fanciful or covered with magical symbols or made out of special material, such as silk. If you attend a gathering of witches, you will probably see a wide range of attire, from magical jewelry to full dress garb, including some fairly outrageous and over-the-top ensembles. It's one of the more entertaining aspects of going to big Pagan conventions, as far as I'm concerned.

When Blue Moon Circle started out, we always dressed up for ritual. We usually wore long dresses or flowing skirts and tops, and we had cloaks for when it got cold later in the year. It is fun to wear the beautiful clothes you rarely get to put on otherwise, and changing into ritual garb can help to put you in the right frame of mind for doing magical work. (Although if you are wearing long dangling sleeves, you will want to take extra care with candles and other open flames.)

The last few years, as we have gotten busier and more stressed (and our older garb no longer fits), we are more likely to just show up in our everyday clothes and be happy to be together no matter what we're wearing.

It can really vary from group to group, but if you are starting out as a new coven or joining an existing one, you should probably discuss whether or not there is an expectation for people to wear garb when attending ritual. There is no right answer for this, just whatever works for the people involved.

Herbs—You might not think of herbs as a tool, but like crystals, many herbs have magical associations and are used in spells as well as included in charm bags, potions, and even kitchen witchery. The great thing about herbs is that many of them can be used for multiple purposes, such as magic, culinary, and healing work. They're the one tool that can be out in plain sight in your kitchen and no one will ever think it means you are a witch—unless you have a jar labeled "Eye of Newt" (which was actually a folk name for an herb). Then they might actually guess.

Incense—Incense comes in a few forms. There are tall sticks, short cones, and powdered resins that are burned on a disk of charcoal. They can be made from natural herbs or artificial fragrances, although I have a strong preference for the natural ones, both because it is closer to the nature magic we practice and because people (me included) are less likely to be allergic to the ones without chemicals. The resins can be very strong and cause a lot of smoke so are best used outside. You can, however, make your own out of any herbs you like, so that's one reason some people like them. Incense can be used to purify the ritual space (depending on its ingredients), create a spiritual mood, or represent the element of air. As with herbs, many people pick a specific scent to go with the intent of the magic being done, but some folks simply have a favorite and use that all the time.

Purifying herbs—A bundle of herbs bound together into a stick or wand or used loose. Sometimes made from white sage (a desert plant related to but not the same as common kitchen sage) but may also include lavender, cedar, sweetgrass, mugwort, rosemary, juniper, or other herbs. The burning smoke is used to cleanse and purify a space or a person. Used both in magic and healing. Alternately, purifying herbs can be thrown on a bonfire or burned in a cauldron or some other firesafe container. Incense can be used instead.

Speaking stick—The speaking stick may be an actual stick or any other item that can be easily passed around the circle. We use a funky crooked stick that came from my yard. It's about two feet long, and we decorated it with ribbons and mystical symbols. But to be honest, if we don't remember to bring it to ritual, we've been known to pass anything from a rock to a candle. The important thing is that whoever is holding the speaking stick is the only person who is actually talking. If people have a lot to say, the stick may make the rounds a number of times.

Staff—A staff is largely ceremonial, and not all witches use them. Essentially a tall, sturdy piece of wood (about the height of a person), it can be used to etch the ritual circle into the ground or simply to guide energy. Blue Moon Circle spent one ritual creating a group staff that holds the focus of everyone involved. We decorated it with beads strung on wire that we wrapped around it, feathers, wood-burned symbols, and more. We occasionally use it for larger, more formal rituals as a way to welcome people into the circle area by holding it across the entrance and then raising it, but mostly we just had a good time making it.

Wand—Like an athame, a wand is primarily used for directing energy and pointing. Wands can be made from wood (there are certain woods that are considered to be the most powerful for magical work, such as apple, alder, and oak, but you can use whatever you like) or metal or even long thin crystals. Some of them are simple—nothing more than a piece of wood that you come across in the forest that speaks to you—and others are ornate. It is really just a matter of preference.

SECTION 3

some types of modern covens

Traditionally covens have usually consisted of a large number of people, but that is not always true. These days there are almost as many different kinds of covens as there are witches, but they tend to fall into a few general categories. Some are casual (these tend to be more open) and some are committed (these are usually closed, or guests are only allowed if invited or brought in by an existing member), although there can be many variations on these themes. There are even covens made up of only two people.

Just for Two

It isn't traditional, but if you want, you can be a coven, whether or not you call it by that name, with only two. My good friend Lisa and her long-time magical partner, K, are a perfect example of a two-person group that has been practicing together successfully for many years. They originally began their practice together in 1998, and both were part of a large Pagan collective and a small Wiccan coven for several years.

When those groups ended, they chose to continue practicing together on their own. Some years they meet for sabbats, others they meet on full moons or new moons; they decide around Samhain each year. If time allowed, they might squeeze in an extra thing, like a new moon on a year when they were observing sabbats.

Originally, they cast the circle, made altars, and did all the things. But over time, as both of their practices became more eclectic and they were both drawn deeper into their explorations of Buddhism, they evolved a looser structure. They also started bringing chairs or stools into circle because our bodies age along with our practice. (Blue Moon Circle has done the same thing.)

Things they regularly do as part of their practice/celebrations— These are all particularly suitable for the two-person group, but many of these would work for larger groups as well:

- LABYRINTH WALKS. They are fortunate to have several lovely outdoor public ones available in their area. In this case, the labyrinths were created by local Unitarian Universalist and Episcopalian Churches in their Northern California town.
- NEW MOON READINGS. Lisa tells me they attempted to continue this over Zoom during the early days of the pandemic, though as life as we all knew it disintegrated, they found adopting a "we'll see" mentality about everything was the kindest possible approach.
- BACK-TO-BACK HEART MEDITATION. Lisa says this is a wonderful way to ground into yourself, Mama Earth, and each other, and she kindly allowed me to share their version of this mini ritual later in the book.
- WITCHY WORKDAYS. Making or renewing home protection pouches (always in the autumn, generally between Mabon and Samhain), making magical oil blends/sprays, wrapping herbal cleansing sticks, dressing candles, etc. Restocking their witch cabinets is one of their regular non-ritual activities. Lisa says it's a great way to be social, magical, and productive all at once.

- **Spellwork as needed.** Candles and flying wish papers were once their go-to choices, but as fire danger continues to increase and be a year-round threat in California, they have shifted to amulets and other less risky options.
- **Beach magic.** Always a favorite with them, and probably the one I envy the most, not having access to a beach where I live here in upstate New York. Lisa says the Pacific Ocean is a power source for both of them, and their late-night empty beach rituals often wind up lasting until the wee hours of the morning because of journeying work, which tends to dive deep on a dark, foggy beach.
- **Journey work.** Guided meditations (which they take turns leading), scrying, trance work, or sometimes a long and intensive reading using tarot and oracle decks.

• • •

I asked Lisa what she thought were the benefits of practicing with only two people, and what, if any, the downsides were. Here is what she said:

> "The perk of having practiced together for over two decades—and fairly exclusively for the last fifteen years—is that we know each other so well and often seem to be on the same curve of the spiral energy-wise. We can say anything to each other honestly and lovingly, there is zero drama, and we can raise energy together with little to no effort. Big ritual gestures, while fun, are no longer necessary. Just the chime of a bell and we are in it. We have only two schedules to juggle, and pre-pandemic, would calendar things out several months in advance. Things are different now, but I'm sure we will come back around to that.

> If there's a pitfall, it's the need to catch up and talk if we haven't seen each other in a while, since we are best friends as well as working partners. We can get caught up in catching up and burn through most of our ritual time if we aren't careful. To combat this, we make a point to reconnect prior to our meet-up, taking time for either a lengthy phone call or tea and a good, long chat a day or two ahead of the ritual to cover the "life stuff" so we don't need to bring it with us. We meet up in silence and hold that until after we've walked the labyrinth or have come fully into ritual space/circle. We hug (post-vaccines) or wave (pre-vaccines) and dive right into the magic, saving the sharing/chatting for after, with cakes and wine, of course. There are some traditions we'd never change!

• • •

As you can see, there is a lot to be said for practicing Witchcraft with one other person, especially if it is someone you know well and feel a strong connection to. But even if you want to start something new and can only find one person to do it with you, it is worth giving it a try. Remember that my own coven started with only three, and even today there are times when only two of us can manage to get together.

There is something special about the intimacy of two people who come together in magical space. There are fewer distractions. You can really focus on the ritual and on each other. It is easier to coordinate times and agree on what kind of magical work you want to focus on.

It is true that there is a special power that is raised when you have a larger group working together—as long as that group really *is* working together and is in sync with each other. But you might be surprised to discover how much magical energy even two people can create together.

The downside, of course, as Lisa mentioned, is it can be easy to be sidetracked into chatting or other distractions. There is also no guarantee that two witches will find their magical styles to be in agreement. But when it works, you can develop a deep, heartfelt bond and the ability to fall effortlessly into the magical rhythm of two people who work together in tandem to create magic.

Two-person groups work well for friends, like this particular example. It is also an option for a couple, especially one who doesn't have close witchy friends to share their practice with or who prefers to keep their magical practice more intimate. I have also known parents who introduced their children to Witchcraft by teaching them within a one-on-one situation, or friends who were taught by a grandparent or other relative. It can also be helpful for people who are in a situation where it is difficult or dangerous to practice openly. You are much more likely to be able to keep your Witchcraft a secret if that secret is shared with only one other person.

Two-person groups can do virtually any ritual that a larger group can do, although sometimes there are elements that need to be adapted slightly. Later in the book I've got a few magical workings that are designed specifically for two. You will note that these are fairly simple rituals, without formal circle casting, calling of quarters, or invoking the God/dess. If you want to add those elements, here is a sample of a two-person circle casting that you can add to any ritual.

Formal Ritual Casting for Two

Supplies: Purifying herbs or incense with firesafe holders. Salt and water in a bowl. Four quarter candles (these can be the traditional quarter colors of yellow, red, blue, and green, or all white or natural beeswax). A candle to represent the Goddess, plus one for the God if desired (silver and gold or white and yellow are traditional, but any colors will do).

Optional: Cakes and ale for the end of ritual.

• • •

The ritual basics section earlier in the book may seem a bit complicated when there are just two of you. Here is a slightly abbreviated version that you can use if you decide you want a formal ritual casting.

• • •

Cleanse the circle or yourselves with the purifying herbs or incense of your choice. Be mindful of the outside world and all those things you might have brought into circle with you, and let them go. If you like, you can also anoint yourselves with a mixture of salt and water.

Join hands or stand opposite each other and hold your hands out in a circle so they are almost touching, and feel the energy running from one person to the other. Say together, "The circle is cast. We are in sacred space between the worlds."

Take turns calling the quarters, starting with east, taking turns so each of you does two. If using candles, it might be easier to put them on an altar table between you than to have them spread out into a circle on the outside, but either way will work.

Invoke that Goddess (and God, if appropriate).

You can skip the ritual intro unless one of you has written up something special to share.

Once you have finished with the ritual, dismiss the quarters as you summoned them, thank the God/dess, and open the circle either by clasping hands and then letting go or by lifting your arms and then dropping them to your side again.

Three or More

—the casual approach—

My daughter Jenn grew up in the small town I currently live near and got her love of Witchcraft from me. I was careful when she was a teen to avoid pushing my beliefs on her, but as an adult they were the choice she came to on her own. In her mid-twenties she was a part of Blue Moon

Circle until she moved away, eventually ending up in San Jose, California, where she currently lives. (Ironically, she fell in love with San Jose after we attended our first large Pagan conference there together.)

Now she practices with a loosely associated group of friends—not a formal coven by any means, but people who know each other and periodically come together in some variation or another. This kind of "coven" is becoming more common as witches are drawn to group practice without having the time or inclination to become a formal coven. She is the person who tends to fall into the leadership position, but it is usually a fairly casual approach.

She started writing and putting on rituals when she met her best friend and ritual partner, E, at one of my ritual workshops at that same conference. Together, they were part of an informal coven for a while with some other friends.

Jenn mostly wrote the rituals unless she and her friends attended larger public rituals. Once they all planned and conducted an Ostara ritual for South Bay Circles. Many of her rituals began with pulling a card from the Fifth Tarot, a deck that has ritual suggestions for every card, and from there she would modify it to suit their purposes. One of the most memorable of these rituals was a Shambala meditation where she led all of her coven mates into their inner castle to find a gift from the deities within themselves.

When she lived in a house with a hot tub in the backyard, Jenn led people through cleansing rituals in the hot tub. When she lived in a communal home with a big backyard and a fire pit, there was lots of dancing around the fire. The rituals she wrote always called on the elements and invoked the Goddess but didn't necessarily include candles to light or other tools. Since she lives in San Jose, the ocean is a reasonable distance away for a ritual. She says, "I love full moons on the beach in Santa Cruz. The ocean is magical!"

Art, oracle deck readings, and dancing are some of her go-to's for ritual. Since she and her friends are urban Pagans without much yard space for planting and Jenn is an artist with all the supplies, it is easiest for them to do a metaphorical planting of seeds to sow their wishes for the harvest. She collects oracle decks, so many of the rituals revolve around oracle readings where those taking part set intentions and ask for guidance from the Goddess. She tends to do those around new or full moons.

I asked Jenn about the positives and negatives of the casual coven. She and E. have since practiced with many other friends over the years, but only the two of them have remained consistent in their magical practice together. Due to the fact that they practice with a variety of different people, Jenn writes rituals based on who will be there, what their common interests are, and where the ritual will be taking place.

Jenn told me,

> "Dancing is our favorite. E. and I dance through life so of course it is a must in our ritual practice. Dancing is a great way to build energy, connect with self, connect with other ritual participants, release energy, and it goes well with any of the sabbats. Our current magical practice is heavily influenced by positive psychology, yoga, meditation, dance, art, and shadow work, as well as evidence-based practices such as gratitude, life purpose, and finding one's strengths.
>
> The disadvantages to the way I practice is that there isn't a lot of room for the deep work because practice is canceled often due to scheduling conflicts or adjusted to accommodate people that are just open-minded folks but not witches. I miss having the energy of a larger dedicated group whose energies are familiar. I still hope for that.

• • •

As you can see, the main theme for practicing with a loosely connected group of people is flexibility. The needs, desires, and level of knowledge may vary greatly from ritual to ritual, and a good leader will prepare rituals that accommodate those variations. If you are going to have this kind of practice, it helps to be able to go with the flow of the situation, and the amount of people coming, while still doing the kind of magical work you find satisfying.

The casual nature of these kinds of gatherings means you are less likely to do formal circle castings, quarter calls, and invocations, although you certainly can if you want to. In general, it probably will be easiest to do a simple circle casting hand to hand or just pass purifying herbs or incense. It is also okay to bypass circle casting altogether unless you are doing powerful work that requires a protective barrier.

The flexibility of this approach to group practice can be both an advantage and a disadvantage. On the positive side, it means you can still practice with others even if you don't belong to (or want to belong to) an ongoing coven. There is a lot of joy and satisfaction to be derived from simply sharing magic with like-minded people. The downside, of course, is the lack of predictability about who will come, knowing if you'll all be on the same page, or being certain if you'll be able to get people together for any particular occasion at all. But for people who like to mix a solitary magical practice with the occasional group ritual, this may be the perfect compromise.

Three or More

—the committed group—

Obviously, this is the more traditional type of coven, although no two are exactly alike. The committed group, whether it is three or thirteen (or any other number), is usually run by one or two people, who are sometimes—but not always—referred to as the high priestess or high priest. The same general bunch of people attend most of the time.

Traditional types of covens may be Wiccan or more eclectic or something in between. More often than not these days, the leader may simply be the individual who founded the group or else the person or people who are willing to take on the responsibility of organizing things and writing the rituals, assuming members don't take turns. They can certainly be a mix of different folks with slightly different beliefs, as Blue Moon Circle is, as long as everyone agrees on how they will practice together.

As I've mentioned before, I started my journey as a witch in a group run by a Wiccan high priestess, who had in turn gotten her initial experience and training in a very traditional Wiccan coven run by a high priestess and a high priest. After about five years in her group, I spent an additional year and a day under her guidance training to become a high priestess in my own right.

In this particular case, that meant leading some rituals in our own group as well as some of the larger public rituals we put on at the local Unitarian Universalist church (including a Yule celebration with about fifty people, which was a blast but a little intimidating at the time), doing some extra studying in books she recommended, and things along those lines. After the year and a day were up, but before I was dedicated as a high priestess, I left that group due to interpersonal conflicts, which are one of the biggest reasons covens fall apart.

And then I waited.

When the time felt right, I had two close friends help me with a self-dedication where I pledged my commitment to the gods as a high priestess. It was powerful and moving but not the traditional Wiccan way of doing things. And eventually, about nine months after I left my first group, I founded Blue Moon Circle with two women I barely knew at the time; both had been solitary witches for many years and neither considered themselves Wiccan. We did full moons on our own and sabbats with an extended assortment of local witches, most of whom I knew from my previous group. Miraculously, we're still together today.

All of this is my way of saying that you don't need to worry about *how* your coven works, as long as it works for you and the people you practice with.

What I've learned, in my long years of practice, is that as long as you have clear communication and everyone is getting what they want out of the group, a coven is likely to be happy and fulfilling for those involved. People will come and go—their lives will change, some move away, some get too busy or decide that Witchcraft isn't the right path for them—but that's okay. Talk to each other about magical goals (like working on focus) and mundane needs (like scheduling issues), and try to find compromises that work well for everyone.

And don't forget to have fun. Witchcraft is a spiritual path that is intended to be practiced with both reverence and mirth. If you can do that and walk into the circle with love and trust, I suspect you will find being in a coven a truly satisfying experience.

Advantages to Being in a Committed Coven

You know what to expect: who you're practicing with, how rituals will be performed, what you need to do and not do. In theory you can plan around the group's schedule (although this may vary from group to group—ours used to be extremely predictable, and these days it is a bit more last-minute trying to pull things together with everyone's insane lives).

If you are lucky, you will end up with a group of people who practice together for years and become like an extended family, although this doesn't happen in all covens. You can grow and evolve in your magical work alongside others and form deep bonds of trust that aren't possible with more casual groups.

Disadvantages to Being in a Committed Coven

If you practice together for a long time, you may have to work harder to keep your magical work from becoming stuck in a rut. There is always the risk of interpersonal conflicts, just as in any family.

In my experience, the three biggest causes of a coven splitting up are if the leaders are a couple and break up or if a leader gets a new significant other and puts that person before the needs of the established members of the group or if there is some kind of power struggle where one member decides they want to lead or have more influence and divides the group.

If the coven is small and doesn't take in new members, it runs the risk of stagnating or disappearing altogether if one or two people leave.

To avoid these things, it is important to establish a few basic ground rules you all agree on from the beginning and keep the lines of communication open so you can make adjustments as needed as you go along.

A Note about Large Covens

Most of the time, groups are made up of anywhere from a few people to as many as a dozen. But there are also larger groups, which may be a permanent situation (a substantial number of people who practice together all the time) or an assortment of smaller groups who come together to practice on occasion.

In Binghamton, which is about an hour from me, there are a number of small covens who belong to a looser larger organization and often join together on one person's land (in nice weather) or the local Unitarian church (in colder months) to celebrate the sabbats together. The rituals may be put on by different covens in turn. Blue Moon Circle and I have attended many of their Beltane rituals and really enjoyed spending the day with a much larger gathering of Pagans than our own little group, even if our usual preference is for small and quiet.

This particular bunch allows attendance by anyone if they are first brought in and sponsored by someone who is already a participant. Other large groups may have open attendance, where anyone can come. In some more populated areas, open rituals may even be posted or advertised and held in public spaces. Usually these are put on by Pagan organizations rather than covens, but as with all things witchy, there are many variations in how things are done.

A large coven is not exactly the same thing as a casual larger group that comes together in a less formal fashion, but any ritual that will work for one will probably work for the other.

In fact, most (although not all) of the rituals in this book will work for a coven of any size with just a few tweaks. There are a few that are specifically designed for a two-person coven or for a much larger gathering, but even these can probably be adapted if they appeal to you but don't fit your exact situation.

SECTION 4

GETTING STARTED

For many people, it is a lot easier to join an existing coven than it is to create one of their own, but sometimes that isn't an option. Maybe there isn't a coven in your area or the only ones that are there are closed groups who aren't currently accepting new members. Maybe you live in a rural part of the country where it can be hard to connect with other witches, so even if there *is* a coven, you might not be able to find it.

Or maybe you've attended rituals at one or more local covens and simply didn't click with the members or their style of practice. Possibly, as with my experience, you were part of a coven run by someone else for a while, and eventually it simply stopped working for you.

In that case, you may want to consider starting your own. As you can see from the preceding section, all you really need is one other like-minded person. Blue Moon Circle started with only three. Maybe you know a bunch of people who want to get together less formally, like Jenn did, and can start with that and see where it goes. No matter which approach you take, there are pros and cons, and only you can decide what is the right path for you.

Deciding to Start Your Own Coven (or Not)

There are a couple of things to consider when deciding whether or not to start a coven, no matter which type it is. Even the most casual groups require a certain level of time, energy, and some ongoing commitment to maintain them. If your life is already full to overflowing, you'll need to figure out whether or not there is room for something else, even if it is only once a month.

Leading (or facilitating) a coven also requires a minimum of organizational skills, people skills, and, in many cases, at least some basic magical supplies. You'll need a place to practice, whether it is your home or elsewhere, and at least one other person to practice with.

You might ponder this question for a while and decide that now isn't the time. Or you might have a bunch of friends who come together and say, "We'd love to do this! Let's go for it."

One thing you can start out with, if you do choose to begin a new coven, is a group dedication. Blue Moon Circle did this when we first came together, and I have always felt it was a wonderful way to formalize our intention to practice magic together. Obviously, if you are going to have a more casual group, you won't want to do this step.

Group Dedication

Unlike a personal dedication, in which you dedicate yourself to the Craft and the gods, this one serves to formalize the commitment of all those involved in the coven. You are binding yourselves together with magic, so this isn't something to be done lightly. But if you are sure your coven intends to move forward together, this is a great way to start forming a connection that will continue to grow stronger over the years.

Note that dedicating yourself to a coven doesn't necessarily mean you are binding yourselves to that group for life. People are allowed to change their minds, and sometimes life moves in ways that are out of our control. Not all covens feel the need or desire for a group dedication, but it can be an amazing bonding experience under the right circumstances.

The original version of this ritual can be found in my first book, *Circle, Coven & Grove: A Year of Magickal Practice* (Llewellyn, 2007). It definitely resonates with my early Wiccan roots, so feel free to change it up in any way that suits your own coven if this feels too traditional for you.

Supplies: A small taper candle for each member of the group (you can all use the same color or you can each have a different color). A large white group candle. Toothpicks or sharp sticks for writing with. A long piece of red yarn. Scissors or a knife. Candles for the four quarters plus one for the Goddess. Purifying herbs or incense. Salt and water in a bowl. Cakes and ale. Copies of the dedication spell for each person.

Optional: A special chalice for group work only. Ritual anointing oil. A box for your yarn to be put into once the ritual is over. A speaking stick.

• • •

This ritual can be led by a high priestess or high priest, the group leader, or different members can take turns speaking. Because Blue Moon Circle used a high priestess at the time, that's how this is written, but feel free to change it up in whatever way works best for your group. If possible, this ritual should be performed on the night of the full moon, although it isn't absolutely necessary. You can also make the ritual less formal if you choose to.

To arrange the ritual: Place all the supplies on an altar table or the center of the space you are using. Quarter candles can be placed in their proper positions on the table or at the edges of the circle. Hand out copies of the spell and individual candles.

• • •

Consecrate and cleanse the space by passing purifying herbs or incense. The leader may say, "We bless and consecrate this sacred space, cleansing and clearing it for magical work."

Consecrate and cleanse the circle by passing salt and water mixed together. You can sprinkle the salt and water on the circle itself, on yourselves, or both.

Cast the circle. This is a powerful and important ritual, so be sure to focus when casting the circle. This is a good time to use a formal casting where the leader walks around the outside of the circle with their athame, a magical broom, or a sage wand. You also can cast the circle hand to hand.

Call the quarters and light the candles for each one.

The leader lights the Goddess candle and invokes the Goddess: "Great Goddess, we—your children—come before you on this, the night of your full moon, symbol of your power and beauty. Be with us tonight and lend us your strength, your wisdom, and your power. Watch over us in this rite as we dedicate ourselves to each other and to you. Welcome, and blessed be."

Leader or coven member: "We have come together tonight for the purpose of dedicating ourselves and this group, ______ (name of group). This rite formalizes our intent to work together as we follow the path of the Old Gods and practice our craft to the best of our abilities. We state our intention to work together in perfect love and perfect trust, for the betterment of all. Are all here so agreed?"

All members should answer: "We are."

Group members can sit for the next part of the ritual. All members are given a colored candle, which they should inscribe (using their athame, a toothpick, or a stick) with their names. They can use their magical names, if they have one, or their mundane names. The large white group candle is passed around the circle, and each member can inscribe it with whatever they feel is appropriate for the moment—names, symbols, runes, etc. The candle can be anointed with a ritual oil (if you have some) and then placed back in the center of the circle.

Once this is completed, everyone should stand again. The next part can be performed by the leader for each person or you can go around the circle and have each member do the next person's.

Use the red yarn to "take the measure" of each group member. Without cutting the yarn, measure off a length equal to the height of that person (if someone is 5 feet tall, you would measure off 5 feet of yarn, so be sure that you have enough when you start). Tie a knot at that spot, then take the measure of the next member. When you are done, you will have a long piece of yarn with as many knots in it as there are group members. You can then cut it off at the end. This piece of yarn represents your group. You can anoint it with oil if you like, and you may wish to keep it in a special box. Pass it around the circle and let everyone hold it for a moment and put energy into it. In later rituals, you can use this length of yarn to mark out your circle space. If you add a new member to the group later on, you can measure out a new length for them and tie it onto the end of the group piece.

When you are finished, spread the piece of yarn out around the inside of the circle so that each person is holding a knot. It doesn't matter if it is their own knot. There will probably be yarn lying on the floor between you, and that's fine.

Holding the yarn in their left hands, the members will take their colored candles and light them off the Goddess candle. Together, the group members will light the white group candle with their individual candles, then blow out the individual candles, leaving the group candle burning. (This may not go as smoothly as it is written—that's okay. Don't forget to laugh at yourselves and have fun, even if things go wrong.)

With all still standing, the leader will lead the group in the dedication (if necessary, you can hold the yarn in your left hand while holding a book or paper with the words in your right):

We are witches
We walk the path of the Old Gods
From this moment forth
We will not walk alone
Together, we will worship
Together, we will practice our craft
Together, we will learn and grow
We vow to work, from this day forward
In perfect love and perfect trust
According to the free will of all
And for the good of all
Creating only beauty
Singing in harmony
Our song upon the earth
Love is the law and love is the bond
In the name of the Goddess and the God
So do we vow, and so mote it be!

Take a moment of silence. If you like, you can pass a hug or a kiss around the circle. Sit.

Pass cakes and ale. These should be something special, and if you want you can serve whatever you are drinking in a special chalice that will be reserved for the group from that time on.

Pass the speaking stick (optional). Each person should take a moment to speak about what is in their heart at that moment.

Dismiss the quarters.

Leader thanks the Goddess: "Great Goddess, mother of us all, we thank you for your presence in our circle at this ritual of dedication. May you continue to watch over us when we are together and when we are apart. Farewell, and blessed be."

Open the circle by clasping hands or raising them to the sky and saying: "The circle is open but never broken."

Creating Permanent Circle Space

Blue Moon Circle has one permanent and one semipermanent circle space, both at my house. Out behind my barn there is a stone circle made up of flat rocks from around my property that we often use when the weather is nice enough to be outside. When we have to be inside, we use my living room, where there is an altar table that is kept up against the wall when not in use. I had a woodworker make me one that is round, with sides that fold down, which is very handy.

I honestly can't remember if we formally blessed and consecrated the outside circle before using it—it was back in 2004, and that's a long time ago! At this point, we've done so much magical work at my house, the whole place feels like sacred space. But if you can, it is nice to have a dedicated circle space that has been cleansed and consecrated to magic.

Depending on whether or not you practice in the same place each time you meet (the coven leader's house, for instance) or use a public space (like a room you rent from a local shop or spiritual organization) or take turns meeting at different members' homes, creating permanent circle space may or may not be a practical idea. But there are always ways to work around these kinds of issues.

For instance, if you can't consecrate a specific space, you can find an altar table that will be usable no matter where you are and treat that as movable sacred space. Alternately, you can create a circle space cloth—anything from a lightweight rug that can be pulled out of a closet at someone's house to a plain sheet or piece of fabric that your coven decorates together or a store-bought witchy-themed tapestry that you can place on the floor in the middle of whatever room you are using for your magical work.

When your group does this simple ritual, if you are using an altar table or a floor cloth (or both) instead of a permanent space, simply set them up as they would be when you use them in the future and focus your intent on instilling the magic of your circle into them in a lasting form.

Supplies: Altar or floor cloth. Four small candles (votive size is good) in firesafe containers; these can be the quarter colors (yellow, red, blue, and green) or white. Two larger candles for Goddess and God in their own containers. Purifying herbs or incense. Salt and water in separate bowls. One gemstone for each person in your group (these can be anything from small tumbled stones to quartz crystals, and they don't have to be fancy or expensive; these can be provided by the group leader or each person can bring their own). Matches.

Optional: Small table to use as an altar if you aren't consecrating one. Decorating tools like fabric paint, markers, etc., if you will be decorating a floor cloth as part of the ritual (you can do this for fun even if you will be using a permanent space, if you like). Cakes and ale.

To arrange the ritual: Set everything up in a circle, with the table or altar in the middle and the optional cloth on the floor. Quarter candles should be placed at the four directions (east, south, west, and north) either at the edges of the space or on the table, and the God and Goddess candles should be on the table with the rest of the supplies except the stones, which should be kept on each member's person until it is time to use them.

• • •

If decorating a floor cloth, do this first. Have fun and don't worry too much about making it perfect. But remember to focus on the fact that you are creating a magical item you will use together for some time to come.

Stand in a circle around the center table or floor cloth. If there are at least four of you, someone should stand at each quarter; otherwise, one person can cover two spots.

To cast the circle, have the leader start by saying or singing the words "sacred space" and continue repeating them as the person to their left chimes in, followed by the person on their left, until you have come all the way around to the leader again. Once you are all saying it together, lift your arms up and then bring them down again. Return to silence. The leader then says: "We are in sacred space between the worlds. Here we are safe. Here our words have power."

Light the purifying herbs or incense and pass it around the circle. Each person should waft the smoke over their body, from head to toe, as well as the area between them and the next person. When the herbs or incense come back to the person who started it (this can be the leader or someone else), they can say, "This circle is cleansed and purified. It is sacred space today and moving forward, and we are all sacred within it."

Call the quarters, starting with east. Light the appropriate candle and say: "We summon the powers of the east, the element of air, to guard our circle and sanctify it for magical work today and moving forward." Repeat with south (fire), west (water), and north (earth).

Invoke the Goddess and God (this can be done by the leader or by two different members). Light the Goddess candle and say: "We invite the Goddess to join us in our sacred space, to guide and bless us, today and moving forward." Repeat for the God.

Relight the herbs or incense. Have a member walk it around the outside of the circle and then place it on the table/altar. They should say: "With the power of air and fire, we bless and consecrate this space for positive magical work."

Have a member walk around the outer edges of the circle, sprinkle the water, and say: "With the power of water, we bless and consecrate this space for positive magical work."

Have a member walk around the outer edges of the circle, sprinkle the salt (you don't have to use a lot), and say: "With the power of earth, we bless and consecrate this space for positive magical work."

Each person should hold their gemstone in one hand in front of their hearts and say together: "With the power of our spirit, we bless and consecrate this space for positive magical work today and moving forward." They should then all step forward and place their stones on the table, then step back.

The leader says: "This is now a sacred space from this day forward. Within it we shall work our magic for the good of all and according to the free will of all."

Everyone says: "So mote it be."

If desired, have cakes and ale.

The stones can be reclaimed by the people who brought them or exchanged so that each person leaves with a different stone than the one they brought. Alternatively, they can be placed in a pouch and kept with the group's magical supplies and used in future rituals.

Thank the Goddess and the God for their presence in circle and dismiss the quarters.

The leader says: "The circle is open but never broken. Merry meet, merry part, and merry meet again."

SECTION 5

CELEBRATING THE SABBATS

The sabbats, the eight holidays on the Pagan Wheel of the Year, are often an important component of a group practice. Not all groups meet for every single one, and there are some that focus primarily on the esbats (full moons) and other phases of the moon, but for most of us, the sabbats are both a reason to get together and a way of celebrating the changing seasons of the year.

Magical work done at the sabbats usually revolves around the various aspects of the season (such as rebirth and new beginnings at the spring equinox) and taps into the specific energy of the holiday.

> Note: If you live in the southern hemisphere, the holidays are reversed because the seasons are reversed—the summer solstice falls in December, for instance—but the sabbats are still the same, just practiced on different dates.

There are two solstices (summer and winter), two equinoxes (spring and fall), and four quarter-cross holidays that fall in between them. Most of these, especially the solstices and equinoxes, can be found in many cultures, some of them dating back to the dawn of human civilization. Observing these special days is another way of celebrating the long history of Paganism and the path that was walked by so many before us.

For Blue Moon Circle, the sabbats are a vital part of our practice together, although we do occasionally have to skip one due to scheduling issues. There are also times when only some of us can get together instead of the entire gang, but if there are at least three of us, we usually go ahead anyway. Rituals can vary from those that are serious and very involved to ones that are simple and brief. We almost always have a feast afterward, with each person bringing a dish to contribute to the feast table.

We like to be outside when possible. In upstate New York, that usually means Beltane through Samhain since there is often snow on the ground from November through March and it is cold, although if it is raining or insanely buggy, we are happy to hide inside. If we can, we light a fire in the fire pit since many Pagan holidays are traditionally also fire festivals.

For almost our entire practice, we have done sabbats as formal rituals, complete with casting the circle, calling the quarters, invoking Goddess and God, and so on. In the past year or two we have mostly become less formal, simply gathering outside around the bonfire and passing the purifying herbs to signal the start of the ritual.

As with every other type of ritual, there is no wrong way to celebrate the sabbats. If your coven is more casual in their approach or has been practicing together for a long time, you will be fine if you leave out the more traditional ritual elements. The only exception to this rule, at least for me, is if you are doing very powerful magic (in which case it is a good idea to have all the reinforcement you can get) or if it's Samhain, when the veil between the worlds is thin and you may want extra protection.

The sabbats are all about connecting with the cycle of nature—a good reminder in this modern world when we are often far removed from the natural rhythms—and about celebrating each phase of the year for its positive aspects. Being able to do this with like-minded witches is one of the great joys of being in a coven.

NOTE: If you are new to the practice of Witchcraft, you may be surprised to see how many of the Pagan holidays have been adopted and altered into Christian or mundane holidays. I have always found this rather ironic and somewhat amusing, but it can also be useful if you are trying to share them with non-Pagan friends.

IMBOLC

Imbolc is a quarter-cross holiday that falls on February 2. It is more commonly known these days as Groundhog Day, which makes sense when you think about the fact that the groundhog is supposed to be predicting the coming of spring. It is actually an ancient Celtic celebration of the first stirring of life under the ground, despite the fact that winter is still firmly with us in many parts of the country. Imbolc is a fire festival and is usually dedicated to Brigid, who is a triple goddess of smithcraft, the arts, and healing.

Rituals on Imbolc often center around creativity, divination, healing, cleansing (of self or home to prepare for the new year ahead), or making plans for whatever path (spiritual or practical) you hope to walk during the seasons to come. This ritual combines the ideas of healing and cleansing in a simple rite that can be performed by any size coven.

Imbolc Healing Fires

Supplies: Large bowl of water (if you can gather this from snow melt or rain or a local water source, that's optimal, but tap water will do if that is all you have). A small towel (paper towels will work in a pinch) for each person. A small votive or tealight candle for each person taking part and a heat-proof plate or plates large enough for them all to be placed on. Purifying herbs in a small metal cauldron or firesafe pottery bowl. Table to act as an altar in the middle of the circle. Four quarter candles (yellow, red, blue, and green or all white/natural). Candles for the Goddess and God (silver/gold or white/yellow or both white). Matches.

Optional: Ritual broom (one which is reserved for magical use). Bell, chimes, drum, or singing bowl. Decorative cloth for the table. Altar decorations suitable for the season. Cakes and ale.

To arrange the ritual: Set up the circle with the table in the middle. The bowl of water should be easily accessible from one side, with the God and Goddess candles in the middle and the plate or plates where the candles will be placed near the bowl of water. The purifying herbs should be on the table, along with the optional cakes and ale. Quarter candles can be either at the outer edges of the circle or on the table in their proper directions (north, south, east, and west). If you are using a broom or a musical tool, those should be given to the coven member who will be using them. Depending on how much space you have, towels can be either placed on or under the table or handed to each participant as they enter the circle. Small votives or tealights should be set to the side and handed out individually. Choose one member of the coven to do this ahead of time, and position them where everyone will walk past them to enter the circle area. You can also choose four people ahead of time to call the quarters or the ritual leader can do them all.

• • •

When everything is ready, whoever is leading the ritual should stand by the altar table. Everyone else should enter the circle and be handed a candle as they do so.

The leader says, "Welcome to our Imbolc ritual. We celebrate the first stirrings of the earth coming back to life, no matter how subtle they may be, and we tap into the season's energy for healing, cleansing, and renewal."

A group member walks around the outside of the circle with the broom or lit purifying herbs as the leader says, "We sweep away the old and cleanse and purify this space for magical use, wafting away old patterns that no longer work and making room for healing and positive change."

The purifying herbs are then passed around the circle from person to person as the leader says, "We cleanse and purify ourselves and make room for healing and positive change."

Leader says, "We cast the circle hand to hand." Leader takes the hand of the person to their left, and that person takes the hand of the person to their left until all in the circle are linked. Leader says, "The circle is cast." All repeat (it is good to have a few people who know this is coming, if you don't do this often, so everyone will get the idea). Repeat two more times. Leader says, "So mote it be."

Call the quarters and light the candles for each one (the leader can do all four at the altar or individual members can call them on the outside of the circle).

Invoke the Goddess and God and light their candles (leader or two members).

Leader: "Today we gather to celebrate Imbolc. Winter is still with us, but beneath our feet, the ground stirs. The seeds begin to think about the possibility of coming to life. A slow, subtle shift has begun, and we can tap into that energy to encourage our own potential for change and growth. Imbolc is sacred to Brigid, a triple goddess of smithcraft, the arts, and healing. During this ritual we will call on her to purify and heal us. (points to bowl of water) First we will use water to cleanse ourselves of old, unhelpful thoughts, habits, or patterns that don't work for us anymore—all those things that keep us stuck. (holds up a candle) Then we will call on Brigid's sacred flame to help us heal and move forward into the year ahead with renewed strength, clarity, and peace. Each of us in turn will come to the altar and place our hands in the water. Then we will light a candle to symbolize our desire for healing. If you wish, take a few moments at the water to visualize all the things you wish to wash away. When you light your candle, think of all the aspects of your life you want to be healed. Then let it be so."

The leader moves to the altar and demonstrates, placing their hands in the water and then using a towel to dry them, then putting their candle on the plate and lighting it. If you are using a bell or some other instrument, the person who has it should ring the bell after each person lights their candle. (When it is their turn, they can hand it to the person next to them who can ring it for them.)

Moving around the circle to the left, each person should come up and take their turn.

When everyone is done, there can be a moment of silence. Then the leader says, "We have washed away the old and invited healing and positive growth. We have started our year with strength and purpose, and so it will move forward. So mote it be."

All: "So mote it be."

Pass cakes and ale. (Optional; if you have a large group, you will probably want to skip this.) If desired, the leader can say a few words to bless them before they are sent around.

Dismiss the quarters.

Thank the God and Goddess.

Open the circle.

Feast!

spring equinox

The spring equinox falls on or around March 21 every year (the dates can vary by a day or so in each direction) and marks the official first day of spring. This sabbat is also sometimes referred to as Ostara, and many of the Christian traditions of Easter were adapted from the Pagan origins of this holiday. It is one of only two days of the year (the other being the autumnal equinox) when there is a perfect balance between light and dark, with day and night being equal in length.

Spring is all about new beginnings and a celebration of the potential that lies ahead. Symbols such as eggs, chicks, and rabbits (fertility, anyone?) all represent life coming back to the earth after the dormant period of winter. The spring equinox is the perfect time to tap into the energy of rebirth and renewal and do magical work to encourage your own new beginnings.

Spring Equinox Seed Bombs

Supplies: Clay (this can be artist's clay, soil heavy in clay if there is some near you, or even unscented clay cat litter that has been moistened ahead of time). Potting soil. Wildflower seeds. Large bowl to mix them all in (if you have a really large group, you can use a bucket). Small slips of paper. Pens or pencils. A table to use as an altar that is large enough to hold all the supplies. Four quarter candles (yellow, red, blue, and green or all white). God and Goddess candles (yellow / cream or gold / silver or white). Purifying herbs or incense. Salt and water mixed in a bowl small enough to pass around the circle. Copies of the spell for each participant. Matches.

Optional: Small paper plates. Altar decorations suitable for the season such as fresh flowers, small stone or chocolate eggs, a cloth in pastel spring colors, etc. Cakes and ale. Damp paper towels or cloths.

To arrange the ritual: Place the altar table in the center of the circle, with God and Goddess candles in the center and any decorations you desire, and the quarter candles either in their proper directions (north, east, south, and west) on the table or at the edges of the circle. Clay, soil, seeds, mixing bowl, and paper plates should be set to one side on the table (if the clay is in a large container, it can go underneath). Pens and slips of paper can be placed on the table or handed out to participants as they enter the circle. Purifying herbs and a bowl of water should also be on the table, along with optional cakes and ale.

NOTE: Depending on the size of your group and how you like to do things, you can either have people take turns coming up to the altar table and fixing their seed bombs there or scooping the ingredients onto a small paper plate and taking them back to where they were sitting, along with pen and paper, so they can all work on their seed bombs at the same time.

• • •

Leader says, "We pass the purifying herbs, which represent fire and air, to cleanse and purify ourselves. Let the smoke carry away our mundane worries and concerns so that we might focus on our magical work." (Herbs are passed around the circle to the left.)

Leader/group member says, "Water and salt represent the elements of water and earth. They wash away any negativity and ground us in this magical space." (Salt and water are passed around the table, mixed together in a bowl. People can anoint themselves as desired.)

Leader says, "The circle is cast. We are between the worlds, outside of time, safe and empowered by the magic we summon here."

Call the quarters and light the candles for each one. The leader can do all four at the altar or individual members can call them at the altar or on the outside of the circle.

Invoke the Goddess and God and light their candles (leader or two members).

Leader or group member says, "Today is Ostara, the spring equinox. It marks the first official day of spring and the beginning of the season of rebirth and renewal. The earth is slowly coming back to life as the light grows stronger and the ground warms. It is a time for new beginnings, for hope, and for magic. In celebration of this, we will be creating magical seed bombs. (holds up a completed sample, which should be about 2 or 3 inches around, and gestures toward ingredients on the table) In case you're not familiar with seed bombs, I promise that the only things they explode with are flowers. Clay and soil are mixed together with seeds, usually wildflowers, and tossed in hard-to-reach places to beautify and bring a touch of nature where there might not otherwise be one. In our case, we will be adding a touch of magic and purpose to our creations because we're witches and we can. Each of you has a piece of paper and a pen. Take a moment to think about what new beginnings you want to set into motion for the seasons ahead. What do you want to achieve that you can plant the seeds for now, whether magical or mundane? When you have these goals firmly in your mind, write them down on your paper. Really focus as you do this, and put all your energy into your intent."

Take time to let people do this. When everyone is ready, move on to making the seed bombs. Depending on whether you are having people take turns or work on them all together, say one of the following:

"Now we will take turns coming to the altar and mixing the ingredients for our seed bombs. When you have your mixture of clay and soil at a consistency that will hold together, add the seeds. Then wrap the entire thing around your slip of paper and form it into a ball. When you have made yours, return to your spot in the circle and hold it in your hands, focusing on the goals you wrote down. When everyone is done, we will say a spell together to activate our magical seed bombs. Later, you can place them in your yard or garden or inside a pot or simply toss them into a spot somewhere outside where you think they will grow and flourish."—**OR**—"Now we will take turns coming to the altar and taking the ingredients for our seed bombs. Return to your spot in the circle and mix the ingredients together until your clay and soil have a consistency that will hold together, then add the seeds. Wrap the entire thing around your slip of paper and form it into a ball. Focus on the goals you wrote down as you do this. When everyone is done, we will say a spell together to activate our magical seed bombs. Later, you can place them in your yard or garden or inside a pot or simply toss them into a spot somewhere outside where you think they will grow and flourish."

When everyone is ready, hold the seed balls and recite the spell together.

Spring is here: the earth awakes
And sets her mind on growing
We too will plant our seeds for growth
Potential true and glowing
All that we wish for, need, and want
Shall flourish in the sun
With these balls of clay and seed
Our magic has begun!

If you want, pass around damp cloths or paper towels so that people can clean their hands.

Pass cakes and ale (optional). If you have a large group, you will probably want to skip this. If desired, the leader can say a few words to bless them before they are sent around.

Pass the speaking stick (optional).

Dismiss the quarters.

Thank the God and Goddess.

Open the circle.

Feast!

Beltane

Beltane, or May Day, is a quarter-cross holiday that falls on May 1, although some observe it starting on May Eve, the night before at sunset. It originated as a Celtic fire festival, and it is associated with fertility, romantic and sensual love, and the beginning of the growing season. People often dance around a maypole, a large pole with a wreath of ribbons hanging down from the top. The participants dance in opposite directions, half going one way and the other half going the other, weaving the ribbons together around the pole, usually with great merriment.

In the Wiccan tradition, this holiday celebrates the union of the God and Goddess, and it is likely that our early Pagan ancestors performed rites to increase the fertility of their fields. The success of the year's planting made the difference between eating or going hungry back in those days, so this was a serious, if joyful, business.

While we don't all necessarily grow crops to survive, we all have things in our lives that we want to grow healthy and strong, whether that is our spiritual practice, our careers, our families, or our relationships. This ritual will tap into the energy of Beltane to encourage our own personal "fields" to be fertile, abundant, and successful, whatever they happen to be.

Note: If possible, this ritual should be done outside under the sun. If you can't be outside (or if the sun isn't shining), just use your imagination.

Supplies: Enough bright, colorful flowers for each participant to get one. Enough votive or taper candles for all to have one (multiple colors are nice, but white is fine), each in a firesafe container or holder; if you have a lot of people, you can ask participants to bring their own. Toothpicks. A table to put the supplies on; if you have an outside circle, you may use a large flat rock. Long strands of ribbons or streamers. Four quarter candles (yellow, red, blue, and green or all white). God and Goddess candles (yellow/white, gold/silver, or both white). Purifying herbs or incense. Matches. Upbeat recorded music (something Pagan or Celtic or the kind of thing you might hear at a Renaissance faire, for example)—you can play this on a CD player or with an iPod connected to a Bluetooth speaker or anything else that works for you; if you are lucky enough to have musicians in your coven, live music is even better.

Optional: Basket to hold the flowers or candles. A bonfire if you can have one. Cakes and ale. Speaking stick. Altar decorations like flowers or some other offering for the gods, a seasonal cloth, crystals, or any items that suit the occasion.

To arrange the ritual: Quarter candles should be placed at the edges of the circle in the proper directions (north, east, south, west). All other supplies should be placed on the table in the center, except the music player, which should be off to the side and out of the way. The baskets or containers of flowers and candles can be either on the table or underneath if there isn't enough room.

Beltane Blessings

Gather in a circle. If you want to be formal, you can process in one at a time. If you are going to have a bonfire, have it already lit, and put the table off to the side.

Leader says, "We pass the purifying herbs/incense, which represent fire and air, to cleanse and purify ourselves. Let the smoke carry away our mundane worries and concerns so that we might focus on our magical work." (Purifying herbs/incense is passed around the circle to the left.)

Leader/group member says, "It is Beltane, and so we rejoice! The flowers bloom and so do we."

Group member says, "We cast the circle with the flowers of summer, each one a gift from nature, each one a blessing from the gods, just as we all are." (Takes a flower from the basket or bundle and then hands the rest to the person to their left so that the flowers go around the entire circle, with each person taking one.)

Leader says, "The circle is cast. We are between the worlds, outside of time, safe and empowered by the magic we summon here. The special magic of Beltane opens our hearts and calls to our spirits, and so we gather together to celebrate this sabbat."

Call the quarters and light the candles for each one (the leader can do all four or individual members can call them).

Invoke the Goddess and God and light their candles (leader or two members).

Leader says, "Today is Beltane, a sacred fire festival dedicated to love and fertility and abundance. Our ancestors danced in the fields to ensure the crops would grow strong and plentiful. They probably did a few other things in the fields as well, but never mind that. They lit bonfires and jumped over them for luck. But don't worry, we won't be doing that either. What we will be doing today is magic to ensure that our own harvests will be successful, whatever it is we are trying to grow or achieve in the season to come. These may be actual crops if you are a gardener, or careers, relationships, spiritual growth, whatever it is you wish to nurture, whatever it is you will be putting your energy and heart into. We will pass around candles to channel the fire aspect of this sabbat, and you can use a toothpick to carve words or symbols onto them that represent your intentions and desires. Dig deep and focus, knowing that you are planting the seeds for that which you desire."

Member walks around the circle handing out candles and toothpicks. People can sit for this portion of the ritual and take as much time as they need to etch words or symbols into their candles.

When everyone is ready, they stand again, holding their candles. The leader says: "It is traditional to dance around the maypole at Beltane. We can't do that, but we can dance within our circle to raise energy to empower our magical work. You can do this in whatever way is comfortable to you. Dance around the circle, dance in place, simply wave your arms in the air, clap, or stamp your feet. Grab a ribbon and wave it through the air. There is no wrong way. When the energy reaches its peak, we will each take turns lighting our candles and sending our desires out into the universe."

The music starts and people dance or stomp their feet, circle around swirling ribbons, or whatever. This continues until the leader feels that the energy has reached its height and turns the music off or down.

Each participant will walk to the table and light their candle with a match or off one of the Goddess or God candles, moving around the circle to the left in an orderly fashion, then returns to stand in their spot in the circle.

Once everyone has done this, the leader says, "Our fire burns strong. Our spirits burn strong. Our Beltane magic is strong and will carry our dreams and desires to harvest. So mote it be."

All (with enthusiasm): "So mote it be!"

Pass cakes and ale (optional).

Pass speaking stick (optional).

Dismiss the quarters.

Thank the Goddess and God.

Open the circle by saying, "The circle is open but never broken. Merry meet, merry part, and merry meet again!"

Feast!

Summer Solstice

The summer solstice, also known as midsummer or sometimes Litha, marks the first day of summer. It falls on or around June 21, although the exact date changes every year. It is the longest day of the year, with the most sunshine and the least amount of darkness. The summer solstice has been celebrated across the world for as far back as we have written history, and it is believed that places like Stonehenge were designed to mark the exact moment of its occurrence. People would travel to these kinds of places or to sacred waters (springs, lakes, rivers) that were said to have special healing powers on this day in particular.

The solstice is a time for rejoicing. The earth is at its most fertile, the sun is full of energy, and light and growth are everywhere. Traditionally this is a common time for handfastings and weddings (the June full moon is sometimes called the Honey Moon) and gathering outside with family and friends. Picnic, anyone?

Blue Moon Circle sometimes uses this sabbat for a more relaxed, informal ritual and invites curious friends or strangers who expressed interest in the group but who we didn't want to include in more focused rituals. Some covens open their rituals to children for the summer solstice, even if they don't normally do so, and make sure that the magic done is kid-friendly. I even know non-Pagans who have summer solstice parties every summer—events that are completely unrelated to Witchcraft but celebrate the history and traditions of the day.

I like to do rituals for the solstice that are both fun and functional, tapping into the powerful energy of sun and earth for healing, growth, and empowerment. Whenever possible, we try to get together outside, wearing cheerful colors under the bright skies, and finish off with a feast of fresh summer foods and maybe even a barbecue.

Summer Solstice Sun Power

Supplies: Bottles of bubbles (you can sometimes find packs of smaller bubble wand favors that are both easier to use and more economical if you have a large number of people). Tumbled gemstones (these don't have to be large or fancy; quartz crystals are nice, but you can use any kind of stone you happen to have or ask people to bring their own and have a few extra on hand in case there are coven members who don't own any). Purifying herbs or incense. Four quarter candles in firesafe holders (yellow, red, blue, and green or all white). Two candles for the Goddess and God in firesafe holders (white/cream or silver/gold or both white). Matches. Table to use for an altar, unless you have a permanent outdoor circle with a flat spot.

Optional: Drums, rattles, or other instruments. Cakes and ale (mead is traditional for the solstice, but any juice will do as well). Speaking stick. Altar decorations like flowers or some other offering for the gods. A seasonal cloth. Crystals or any items that suit the season; they should be bright and cheerful.

To arrange the ritual: Place the quarter candles at the outside edges of the circle in the proper directions (north, east, south, west). All the other supplies should be on the altar table, along with any decorations you wish to use for the occasion.

• • •

All participants gather in a circle. Pass the purifying herbs or incense and have each person waft the smoke from head to toe. The leader says, "With this sacred smoke, we cleanse and clear ourselves of everyday concerns and prepare ourselves to be fully present in this magical space."

Cast the circle hand to hand, starting with the ritual leader taking the hand of the person on their left. Leader says (then all repeat), "We cast this circle hand to hand. Together in magic, together we stand."

Call the quarters.

Invoke the Goddess and God.

The leader says, "We gather today for the summer solstice. It is the longest day of the year, with the shortest night. For this brief moment in time, the light reigns supreme. The sun is powerful overhead; the earth beneath us bursting with energy and abundance. The birds and the animals and the plants all rejoice, and so do we. Therefore, we will do a ritual that taps into that summer energy so we can channel it into whatever we need—healing, prosperity, love, and much more. And we too will rejoice and send our wishes out into the world to be carried on the wind in the form of sacred water and air, flavored with the unlimited potential of childlike enthusiasm."

Have someone hand out the stones or pass them around the circle for people to choose one, or have people take theirs out if they brought them from home. The leader (or some other coven member—this speech can be shared out among a couple of people if you like) can hold up their stone to the sky and say: "Above us is the sun. It is bright and glorious, and its light and warmth enable the plants to grow and the crops to burst forth in the fields. From the sun comes energy and light. (holds stone toward the ground) Below us is the earth. It grounds us and holds us safe. From the earth comes abundance and strength. (holds the stone out in an open palm) Open yourself to the power of the sun and the earth, open yourself to the magic of the solstice, and let the essence of the day be absorbed into the stone you hold, so you may tap into it later when you need it." (If people will be drumming or using rattles, etc., they can either take turns so each gets a chance to use their own stone or play the music one-handed while holding their stone out in the other.)

When the energy in the circle reaches its peak, the leader can hit a drum or say loudly, "So mote it be!"

All: "So mote it be!"

Leader (or other member) says, "Tuck your stone away someplace safe because now it is time to rejoice. We rejoice in the day. We rejoice that we are together. And we revel in the magic and mirth of summer's arrival. (hands out bubbles or passes them around the circle until everyone has some) We will each take turns blowing bubbles into the sky. As you blow, make a wish or as many wishes as you want and let the bubbles carry your wishes out into the universe and up to the gods. You can shout your wishes out loud or keep them to yourself, if you so choose. Put all the force of your will and intent into your breath as you blow, and channel a bit of the summer energy we just collected. And don't forget to have fun!"

Each person takes turns blowing bubbles and sending out their wishes. When the last one is done, all shout together, "So mote it be!"

Pass optional cakes and ale. The leader may say a blessing over them before sending them around the circle; first the cakes: "Bless these cakes, gifts of the earth, that they may nourish our bodies and our spirits, and ground us after our magical work." Then the ale: "Bless this ale; may our lives be as sweet as the fruit in this cup."

Pass speaking stick (optional).

Dismiss the quarters.

Thank the Goddess and God.

Open the circle by saying, "The circle is open but never broken. Merry meet, merry part, and merry meet again!"

Feast!

Lammas

Lammas is the first of three harvest festivals on the Wheel of the Year. It is also known by its Celtic name of Lughnasadh, after Lugh, the god of light. It falls on August 1. Harvest festivals were extremely important to our

Pagan ancestors since a good harvest could mean the difference between life and death or, at the very least, a long, lean winter.

This holiday in particular celebrates grain, and its rituals may incorporate bread, sheaves of wheat, or grains in some other form. It is particularly appropriate to call on deities associated with the harvest, such as Demeter (or Ceres, as she was known to the Romans) and Lugh himself.

Harvests can be metaphorical as well as physical, and you don't need to have a farm or a garden to reap what you have sown. Lammas is a good reminder for us to check in on our goals for the year (both magical and mundane) and see if we have been spending enough time and energy on those things that are truly important to us to help them grow and flourish. If the answer is no, it is still early enough in the season to regroup and get back on track.

This simple ritual is partially a celebration of the harvest and partially an opportunity to check in with the gods and your own wise inner voice to get an answer to that question.

Harvest Wisdom and Guidance

Supplies: A round loaf of bread, preferably the rustic type (it is okay to substitute something gluten-free). White votive candles (enough for all). Some form of divination (this can be tarot cards, rune stones, oracle cards—whatever your coven is comfortable with or you happen to have). Purifying herbs or incense. Four quarter candles in firesafe containers (yellow, red, blue, and green or all white). Goddess and God candles in firesafe containers (white / cream or silver / gold or both white). Copies of the spell for everyone. A table to use as an altar. Matches.

Optional: Cakes and ale. Speaking stick. Altar cloth and decorations suitable for the holiday.

To arrange the ritual: Place the altar table in the middle of the circle. All the supplies can go on it, with the exception of the quarter candles, which should be placed at the proper directions at the outside of the circle (north, east, south, west) if you don't want to have them all on the altar or there isn't room.

• • •

Light the purifying herbs or incense and pass around the circle to the left. The leader can say, "With this sacred smoke, we cleanse and purify our bodies and spirits, entering into the harvest season with clear minds and open hearts."

To cast the circle, pass the bread around (to the left). The leader says, "We cast our circle with the bread of life, symbol of this harvest holiday. As we share this bread, so do we share sacred space and the magic that takes place within it. So mote it be." Each person breaks a small piece off the bread and eats it, then passes the bread to the next person until it goes all the way around the circle.

Call the quarters.

Invoke the Goddess and God.

This next part can be done standing or with everyone sitting comfortably. The leader says, "We gather today to celebrate Lammas, the first harvest festival on the Wheel of the Year. At this point in the cycle, we all hope to be starting to reap the harvest from whatever we planted in the beginning of the year. This might be plans for careers or relationship goals or new directions on our spiritual path. If things are going our way, we might wonder if we could be doing more. If we aren't seeing the results we'd hoped for, we might wish for guidance on how to change that. So we are going to do a little Lammas divination. Fix in your mind the question you wish to ask, and we will pass these cards (or runes or whatever you are using) around the circle. Each person will take one and see if it helps clarify their situation. If you aren't sure what it means, don't hesitate to ask for input from others. Sometimes others can see the answers to our situations more clearly from the outside than we can from the inside."

Pass the divination tool around the circle and have each person ask their question (silently or aloud, as they choose) and see if the cards or runes can give them some guidance. Help each other if asked to and make sure to be supportive and not critical.

Once the divination portion of the ritual is done and the tools are returned to the altar, pass out a white candle to everyone. The leader (or another member) says, "We all have hopes and dreams for the rest of the year. It is not too late to reap those things we wish for and work on creating positive changes in our lives. If you got answers to your questions, focus on that new knowledge and where it can lead you. If you are still seeking clarity, focus on that desire. When we are all ready, we will light our candles and recite this spell together, with the goal of achieving the best possible harvest before the coming of the cold and dark.

Gods of sun and light above
Goddesses of growth and love
Help us with the crops we plant
Our wishes and desires grant
Guide our hearts, keep focus deep
So harvests plenty shall we reap!

"Focus on the candle flames for a few minutes and then blow them out. You can take them home and put them on your altars or somewhere else safe and light them again when you feel as though you need a boost or a reminder of what you are working toward."

Pass cakes and ale (optional).

Pass speaking stick (optional).

Dismiss the quarters.

Thank the Goddess and God.

Open the circle. If you are outside, you can pass the remainder of the loaf back in the other direction, with everyone crumbling a little bit to leave for the birds and other creatures. Say, "Our circle is open but never broken. Merry meet, merry part, and merry meet again!"

Feast!

mabon

Mabon, also known as the autumn equinox, falls on or around September 21 and marks the first official day of fall. It is the second of the three harvest festivals. Depending on where you live, the shift from summer to autumn may be more or less obvious. Here in upstate New York, the changes are unmistakable. The nights grow cooler, the leaves begin to change colors, vacations have ended, and school has started up again.

Even the energy in the air is different: still vibrant but slowing from summer's hectic pace as we prepare ourselves for the quieter months that lie ahead. Today, as on the spring equinox, the light and dark are equal. But from now on, the days grow shorter and the nights grow longer. Mabon is a good time to take a moment to pause and take a deep breath, appreciating what lies behind and what is still to come.

Blue Moon Circle almost always takes advantage of this rare day—only one of two during the year when the world itself is in balance—to work on balance within ourselves. Let's face it: in today's hectic world, that can be hard to find. A little magic to help you out can't hurt.

Mabon Balancing Act

Supplies: Black and white votive candles (one each for everyone). Toothpicks. An apple and a sharp knife on a plate. Purifying herbs or incense. Four quarter candles in firesafe containers (yellow, red, blue, and green or all white). Goddess and God candles in firesafe containers (white / cream or silver / gold or both white). Copies of the spell for everyone. A table to use as an altar. Matches.

Optional: Drumming or other quiet meditative music to play in the background. Basket to hold the black and white candles. Cakes and ale. Speaking stick. Altar cloth and decorations suitable for the holiday.

To arrange the ritual: Place the altar table in the middle of the circle. All the supplies can go on it, with the exception of the quarter candles, which should be placed at the proper directions at the outside of the circle (north, east, south, west) if you don't want to have them all on the altar or there isn't room. The plate with the apple and the knife should be near where the leader will be standing. If you choose, the black and white candles and a toothpick can be handed out to people as they enter the circle. Otherwise they can be given out during the ritual. (If you have a lot of people, the first approach might be easier.)

• • •

Light the purifying herbs or incense and pass it around the circle to the left. The leader can say, "With this smoke, we cleanse and purify our bodies and spirits, entering into sacred space with clear minds and open hearts."

Cast the circle hand to hand. The leader takes the hand of the person to their left and says, "We cast the circle hand to hand," and so on around the circle until it returns to the leader, who says, "The circle is cast; we are between the worlds."

Call the quarters.

Invoke the Goddess and God.

The leader says, "We have gathered together to celebrate the autumnal equinox, also known as Mabon. As the second harvest festival on the Wheel of the Year, it is a time for celebration and gratitude. It is also a time for introspection as we begin to prepare for the colder, darker days ahead. Today the day and night are equal—in perfect balance. Life is sweet and magical, like this apple, a symbol of the harvest season. (slices apple in half across the middle, revealing the pentacle within it, and holds it up so all can see) You see? Even nature has its witchy side, with a pentacle inside each apple." You can use the apple for the cakes portion of cakes and ale later, if you want, cutting it into smaller pieces and passing it around.

Leader continues, or some other member says, "But balance is not always too easy to find. For many of us, it can be an elusive goal. Too much work and not enough relaxation. Too much sitting and not enough movement. Too much sadness and not enough joy. Too much giving and yet getting little in return. Today we will do magical work to help us achieve better balance in our lives, tapping into the special energy of this magical holiday to help us bring that balance into our lives."

If you are using music in the background, turn it on now. If they weren't given out before, pass out black and white candles and toothpicks.

Leader or some other member says, "Nothing in life is completely black or white, and all things have their purpose, but better balance can help us be happier and healthier.

Take your toothpick and carefully etch into your black candle a few words to represent those things that you would benefit from having less of in your life. Then carve into the white candle those things you could use more of. There are no right or wrong answers, just what works for you."

Give people time to complete this thoughtfully. Then continue. "Now we will light our candles. When they are all lit, we will say the spell for balance together." If there are enough matches for everyone, you can light your candles at the same time. If not, pass the matches around the circle until everyone has lit theirs, then recite the spell.

Nature's blessing of the season
Power from the gods above
Bring balance to my life and living
Balance to both mind and love
Work and play in equal measure
Healthy food and restful sleep
All those things I need to prosper
Balance in my life I will keep!

Sit for a minute to take in the power of the spell, then blow out both candles. Turn off music if you used it.

Leader says, "Take these candles home with you and put them on your altar or somewhere else safe. Light them whenever you feel the need to reconnect with this day's energy for balance, and say the spell again."

Pass cakes and ale (optional).

Pass speaking stick (optional). If people want, they can talk about which things they asked for more or less of in their lives.

Dismiss the quarters.

Thank the Goddess and God.

Open the circle. You can say, "Merry meet, merry part, and merry meet again!"

Feast!

Samhain

For many witches, Samhain is the most sacred day of the year. Known to most as Halloween (which was taken from the Christian holiday of All Hallow's Eve, which was in turn adapted from the Pagan traditions that inspired it), it is associated with ghosts and witches and all things mystical and magical.

Samhain, which falls on October 31, is the time when the veil between the worlds (our world and that of those who have gone beyond) is said to be the thinnest. It is a time to reach out to those we have lost and say anything that feels as though it needs to be said, even if it is something as simple as "I miss you." This sabbat is often associated with divination, although you will want to be more cautious than usual about casting a magical circle to keep you safe. It is also the third and final harvest festival, so the altar may be decorated with gourds, pumpkins, apples, and other seasonal fruits and vegetables.

This holiday is sometimes referred to as the witches' New Year. In the calendar of the Wheel of the Year, it is both the last day of the old year and the first day of the new year. Because of this, it is a good time to do a two-part ritual, the first half devoted to saying goodbye to the old year and all that it brought (both good and bad) and the second half opening up to the potential of the new year that lies ahead.

There is some serious energy in the air on Samhain, so even if you normally include children or non-witchy friends in your rituals, this might be a good one to reserve for practicing witches. On the other hand, I was introduced to the Craft at a Samhain ritual, so you never know. Just keep in mind that Samhain rituals can be intense and very powerful, and not everyone will be comfortable with that.

This ritual is a little more formal than most, in keeping with the importance of the night, but that doesn't mean you can't have fun. After all, it is a New Year's celebration too. Blue Moon Circle usually has a solemn beginning followed by a more joyful and high-spirited second half, and this ritual is based on the kind of things we do.

Even if you don't wear garb the rest of the year, Samhain is the one sabbat when you might want to pull out your witchiest clothes, put on your pentacle necklace, and go a little wild. If at all possible, this is a good ritual to hold outside. If you can, it is a wonderful night to have a bonfire. Whether or not you dance around it is entirely up to you.

Spirited Samhain Celebration

Supplies: Black candles (white is okay if you don't have black; tealights or even small chime tapers work well—you want at least one for every person taking part, and if you have a smaller group, you can have more than one for each). Firesafe plate or plates for the candles or a cauldron or shallow dish filled with sand (if you are using sand, you can either rest the candles on top; if using small tapers, poke them down into the sand). A small separate table to put these on unless your cauldron is large enough to rest on the ground. Fresh rosemary sprigs (you can usually find these in the herb section of the grocery store if no one in your group has a garden; if necessary, you can substitute dried rosemary, although it will make more of a mess) and a bowl to put them in. A bell, gong, singing bowl, rattle (or anything that makes a noise); if you don't have any of these, you can create your own rattle by putting dried beans into a jar, although a bell is preferable. Dried corn leaves or pieces of paper and markers to write on them (the corn leaves are very seasonal, and you may be able to find stalks of corn at a farmer's market for decoration or else you can buy corn on the cob at the store, strip the leaves off, and let them dry, using the corn for the feast—otherwise plain old paper will do). A large bowl to put the leaves/paper into if you won't be using a bonfire. Purifying herbs or incense. Four quarter candles in firesafe containers (yellow, red, blue, and green or all white). Goddess and God candles in firesafe containers (white/cream or silver/gold, or both white or both black). Copies of the spell for everyone. A table to use as an altar. Matches.

Optional: Drumming or other quiet meditative music to play in the background. A basket to hold the black candles. Another basket to hold the corn leaves or paper and pens. Cakes and ale. Speaking stick. Altar cloth and decorations suitable for the holiday. If people want to, they can place pictures or symbols of their beloved dead (human and animal) on the smaller altar table with the candles.

To arrange the ritual: Place the altar table in the middle of the circle. All the supplies can go on it, with the exception of the quarter candles, which should be placed at the proper directions at the outside of the circle (north, east, south, west) if you don't want to have them all on the altar or there isn't room. The candles should be placed on the second table along with some matches and anything anyone in the coven wants to put there in memoriam. Bell, gong, singing bowl, or rattle should also be on that table. If using a bonfire or fire pit, light it before the ritual starts. (Make sure you have a bucket of water handy in case of sparks.)

• • •

Pass the purifying herbs/incense around the circle, moving to the left. Be especially thorough in wafting the smoke from head to toe. The leader says, "On this sacred night, we clear and cleanse our bodies and our minds so that we enter this space ready to embrace magic and spirit."

Have the leader or some other member walk around the outside of the circle with a broom (one dedicated to magical work), an athame, or the purifying herbs/incense. As they walk, they say, "I cast this circle round and round from earth to sky, from sky to ground. I conjure now this sacred space outside of time, outside of place. The circle is cast. We are between the worlds, safe and protected."

Call the quarters.

Invoke the Goddess and God.

The leader says, "Tonight is Samhain, the witch's New Year. It is the end of the old year and the beginning of the new. Tonight the veil between the worlds is thin. Tonight we may speak to our beloved dead, knowing that they can hear us more clearly than usual. So we gather together in this safe and sacred space to mourn, to remember, to send love out with open hearts. Each one here will have a chance to light a candle on the altar. (gesture to the smaller table) You can say goodbye to anyone you lost in the past year or in the years before. You might also let go of any dreams that didn't come to fruition or any other kinds of losses. This year is ending. Now is the time to let go of regrets and acknowledge those things we cannot change. When it is your turn, take some rosemary and place it on the altar for remembrance. Then light your candle and speak your losses either silently or aloud, whichever you are comfortable with. When you are done, ring the bell (hit the gong, shake the rattle) to send them out into the universe."

Each person should take their turn. When everyone is finished, the leader or some other member says, "And so we have said goodbye to the old, leaving us free to embrace the New Year and all the potential it holds. For every moment of darkness, there is a moment of light. For every door that closes, there is the possibility for a new beginning. And so we welcome in the New Year, and the wheel turns again."

Hand the corn leaves or paper and pens around the circle (if they are in a basket, just pass that around; if not, someone can walk around and give one to each person). The leader or some other member says, "It is the end of the old year, but it is also the beginning of the new one. We turn our gazes forward and concentrate our energy on what lies ahead. Take a few minutes to think about what you hope to achieve in the season to come and the seasons that follow it. Then write these goals and wishes down."

After everyone has written their goals on the leaves or paper, this person or another continues. If you don't have a bonfire, give them the second set of instructions. "Now that we have set down our goals and our focus is clear, each of us will take turns throwing them into the bonfire, where the smoke will carry our wishes up to the gods"—**OR**—"Take the goals you have written down and fold them up. Hold them close to your heart as we recite this spell, then take them home and put them on your altar, under your pillow, or someplace safe."

Recite the spell together. When you are done, ring the bell/ gong one last time.

We bid goodbye to the year behind
And open our hearts to the year ahead
Gifts and blessings we hope to find
In the weaving of Fate's bright thread
Witches tonight and witches tomorrow
We walk the path with heads held high
Together in joy and also in sorrow
We send our wishes to the Samhain sky
Blessed New Year to all
So mote it be!

Pass cakes and ale (optional).

Pass speaking stick (optional). If people want, they can talk about anything that moves them.

Dismiss the quarters.

Thank the Goddess and God.

Open the circle. You can say, "Merry meet, merry part, and merry meet again!"

Feast!

Yule

Yule, also known as the winter solstice, falls on or around December 21. It is the official start of winter, although in many places that season has already been with us for quite some time. The winter solstice is the shortest day of the year and the longest night, and yet we celebrate the returning of the light, for every day that follows brings with it just a little bit more daylight than the one before.

Many Yule traditions were adopted by Christianity when it moved into Europe, where the winter solstice was sometimes called by that name in Germanic and Scandinavian countries. The Christmas tree comes from the practice of bringing trees and green boughs into the house to symbolize the vibrancy of life in the midst of a time when most growing things are dead or dormant. The red and green colors so familiar to most of us are derived from mistletoe and holly berries, and the star on the top of Christmas trees has five points.

Even the bearded gentleman bringing gifts bears a strange resemblance to the Oak King, who is said to overthrow the Holly King on the day of the winter solstice. There are also many mentions of Yule and Yuletide in popular carols, too. In the mythology of the Wheel of the Year, the Goddess in her role as Mother gives birth to the infant God, bringing light and hope back into the world, thus completing the cycle of birth, growth, death, and rebirth.

There are actually some benefits to all this commonality between Christianity and Paganism when it comes to this holiday. For the people who were raised in a conventional Christian household, as so many were, there may be an element of comfort to the familiarity of overlapping traditions. For those of us who share our lives with non-witches, Yule is one of the few sabbats that lends itself to including them in our celebrations (even if it means leaving out some of the more Pagan and magical bits).

Blue Moon Circle has always skipped the formal ritual on Yule and opted instead to have a Yule dinner party that included spouses and children (for those who had them) and sometimes close friends, some of whom wouldn't have felt comfortable attending a strictly witchy event. For us, being together has always been magic enough.

The ritual that follows is mellow and non-threatening enough to consider inviting friends or family to, if you want to give them a taste of how you practice your spiritual beliefs in a way that hopefully won't make them uncomfortable. You can always skip the circle casting, quarter calls, and Goddess/God invocation if you want. Or you can choose to celebrate with just coven members, put on your fanciest garb, and welcome the returning light in style. As always, it is completely up to you.

A Yuletide Merry

Supplies: Small pine or fir tree/bush (you can often find table-top versions at your local grocery store at this time of year, or if you live in a house where you have a Christmas tree, you can use that; in a pinch, a large potted plant will do). A table to use as an altar. A red candle in a firesafe container or a battery-powered candle (if you have a larger group and are worried about passing around a live candle). Sturdy paper cut into the shape of stars and strung on ribbon or string so they can be hung on the tree (a hole punch makes this easier—if you have a crafty group who enjoys making things, you can cut these out and make them as part of the ritual instead of having them done up ahead of time). Pens. A copy of the spell. Purifying herbs or some seasonal incense such as cinnamon or orange. Four quarter candles (yellow, red, blue, and green or all white). A tall white candle for the Goddess and a short white one for the newborn God. A large white or yellow candle. Matches. Each person attending should bring a small inexpensive wrapped gift that would be suitable for anyone (these can be useful things like nice candles or soap, a pretty crystal, chocolate, or even something homemade like jam or cookies).

Optional: A fancy stand or plate for the large white candle. Decorations for the tree / shrub (these can be fun natural things like cranberries or popcorn to string on a wire, cinnamon sticks, etc., or they can be regular tinsel and tiny ornaments like stars and moons if you can find them). A basket to put the stars and pens in. Plastic or paper bag for cleaning up. Cakes and ale. Speaking stick.

To arrange the ritual: The tree should be in the center of the circle, with the altar table a little to one side. Everyone's wrapped small gifts should be placed around the bottom of the tree. Quarter candles can be placed on the table or around the edges of the circle in their proper directions (north, east, south, west), and the Goddess and God candles, the large white candle, and purifying herbs or incense should be on the table. The paper stars can be placed in a basket with the pens (this can go under the table until you need it if there is no room on top). Copies of the spell can be on the table or given out to people as they enter the circle.

• • •

Gather in a circle. If you want, you can hand out the spell at this time.

Pass the purifying herbs or incense around the circle going to the left. The leader says, "We clear and cleanse this circle and ourselves so we might enter into this sacred space free of negativity and open ourselves to the joy and peace of the winter solstice."

Pass the red candle/battery powered candle. Leader or other member says, "On this day we celebrate the returning of the light, so we cast the circle with this candle, a symbol of the sun and of spirit." As the candle is passed, each person says to the person they hand it to, "May your life be filled with light." When it has made its way around, the person who started it says, "The circle is cast; we are in sacred space."

The leader says, "Today is the winter solstice, a day that has been observed by many cultures throughout the years. It is the longest night of the year and the shortest day. But every day from here on out, there will be a little more sun and a little less darkness, and so we celebrate the returning of the light, which brings with it hope and renewed energy." Light the large candle. "All hail the returning of the sun!" (Everyone repeats, "All hail the returning sun!")

Leader or other member says, "Like many of the other holidays that are observed at this time of year, we often celebrate Yule with the exchange of gifts. For this ritual, we will be doing this in two ways. We will begin by passing out paper stars and some pens. On the stars, write a wish you would like to give to someone in the year to come. This can be anything from prosperity to healing to love. It can be peace or new adventures, courage, growth, faith, or clarity. As we pass the stars around the circle, think for a moment of what you would want to be gifted and what you would gift to others if you could. Then choose a word or phrase and write it on your star." (Pass stars and pens around the circle. Everyone writes in silence. Then collect the stars and pens when everyone is done, and have a group member mix up all the stars and hang them on the tree with the blank side out.)

Leader or another member says, "First we will each go to the Yule tree and choose a gift from underneath, starting with the person to my left. Pick your gift, then go back to your place in the circle. If by some chance the last person left ends up with the thing they brought, they will exchange it with someone at random. Then we will go around the circle and see what the Oak King, working through our companions this day, has gifted us with."

Everyone takes turns going to the tree to pick out a wrapped gift, then go around the circle and each person will open theirs. You may want to have a member go around after this part is finished and collect any wrapping paper and mess in a bag. This part should be done with much joy and merriment.

Once this part is done, the leader or another member says, "As much as we all love to receive gifts that we can hold in our hands, it is important to realize that this season is about a lot more than that. It is about peace, love, and the rebirth of hope. It is about looking forward to the year that lies ahead and embracing the possibilities that come along with the returning of the light. Each of us will now walk up to the tree and pick a star. On that star is a wish, a prayer, a goal, an aspiration, or maybe even a message from the gods—an entirely different kind of gift. If, by some chance, you happen to pick the one you wrote, you can either put it back and pick another or choose to keep it. Read the word or words on the star out loud and then return to your place in the circle."

Each person takes a turn picking a star and reading what it says. You might want to pause for a moment of silence when this is done and let all the messages sink in. Then the leader or some other member says, "We have all received two gifts: one an actual physical gift and one a wish for the future. This circle is filled to the brim with positive energy and love. If only we could share the joy we feel with the entire world. Of course, that would take a much bigger circle! Instead, we are going to read this short spell together—really, less of a spell than a blessing and a prayer. So take a moment to appreciate what we have had here in this sacred space, and then we will recite our blessing together and send it out into the universe as our gift to others."

Bless the day and bless this night
Bless the bright returning light
May all the world feel joy and peace
Love and health that never cease
May each receive the gifts they need
And spread their joy with word and deed
All hail the returning light!

Pass the cakes and ale (optional).

Pass the speaking stick (optional). People may want to talk about whether or not their star word had any particular significance to them. It is surprising how often it does.

Dismiss the quarters.

Thank the Goddess and God.

To open the circle, the leader can go to the table and snuff out the large candle, saying, "This candle is out, but the light that is cast remains. And so our circle is open, but the joy within is still with us. The circle is open but never broken. Happy Yule!"

Feast!

Section 6

Celebrating the Full Moon and the Lunar Cycle

The moon has always had a great significance for those who practice Witchcraft. It is seen as a symbol of the Goddess, and its waxing and waning cycles are associated with her changing aspects of Maiden, Mother, and Crone. The beauty and magnificence of the full moon touch many, but for witches it is a sacred night full of power and magic.

Some witches only practice magic on the night of the full moon. Others also use the different energies of the dark moon, the new moon, or the entire lunar cycle. As with everything else witchy, there is no wrong way. In general, however, the waning moon (after the full moon and until the new moon) is used for magic that deals with decrease, or things you want to be rid of, as the moon grows smaller. The waxing moon, as the moon grows more visible from the new moon until right before the full moon, is used for increase, or things you want more of, as the moon grows larger.

The dark moon, when the moon isn't visible at all, is sometimes used for banishing, but it is also good for meditation, inner work, cleansing, and divination. Some witches choose not to do any magic at all at this time. The new moon, when the first sliver of light appears, is great for new beginnings and starting magical workings that will go through the entire month.

The full moon is considered to be the most powerful time of the month, and many witches save their most important magical work for then. While the full moon is technically only one night, many magical practitioners consider its energy to be in force for two days before and two days after, so don't panic if you can't get to a spell right on that night. (This rule also applies to the sabbats, which is handy if your group wants to get together but can't make it on a Tuesday.)

You can vary your full moon practice to keep it in tune with the changing seasons if you like. In the spring use newly blossoming flowers as part of your ritual, for instance, and in the fall do a full moon magical working with a pumpkin and pumpkin seeds. If you are a crafty witch, the full moon is the perfect time to create charm bags or herbal bath mixes or magical oils, imbuing them with the power of the moon and the Goddess it represents.

If your coven only meets once a month, you might want to consider doing it on the full moon if you can. It is an especially witchy night, and you will likely feel the increase in energy even more when you work with a group.

The following are some simple lunar rituals you can do with a coven of any size. You can do a complete formal ritual if you like—casting the circle, calling the quarters, and so on—or you can skip those steps and dive right into the ritual if your group would rather do that. Remember that for lunar-focused magical work, we usually invoke only the Goddess, not the God. This is her night and her magic.

Full Moon Ritual 1

—goddess celebration—

If at all possible, full moon rituals are best performed outside once the moon has risen and you can see it in the sky. There are lots of things that can make this difficult: the weather, a need for privacy, lack of a good outdoor ritual space, or even voracious witch-eating mosquitoes. Blue Moon Circle is located in upstate New York, so outside rituals rarely take place in the winter months and we are periodically rained out when it is warmer. Still, if you can, being able to be outside and look up at the moon is a wonderful thing.

However, if you can't be outside, simply use your imagination. Whether or not you are right out underneath it, the full moon is still there and the energy is just as powerful.

Supplies: White candles (one for each person) in firesafe containers that won't be too hot to hold. Large white or silver Goddess candle. Flower petals as offering to the Goddess (rose petals or lavender or even whatever flowers happen to be growing in your yard). Purifying herbs or incense. Matches.

Optional: Copies of the chant. Small table to use as an altar. Cakes and ale.

To arrange the ritual: Bring all your supplies outside and stand under the moon in a circle. Each person should have a white candle and a bowl or handful of flower petals. The Goddess candle can be on a table or else the ground in the middle of the circle, along with the optional cakes and ale.

Note: The coven leader can do everything here, or various members can take part. Just be sure, if you are doing it that way, that everyone knows what they are supposed to say or do and when.

• • •

Pass the herbs or incense around the circle for cleansing and purification as well as a reminder that you are now entering sacred space. This can be done silently.

Leader says, "We gather here on the night of the full moon to worship the Goddess."

Leader (or other) says, "We gather as witches to revel in the power of the moon."

Leader (or other) says, "We gather with the purpose of channeling that power into ourselves so that we may use it to fuel our magical work."

All: "So mote it be, and so it is."

Leader (or other) says, "We light this candle to honor the Goddess, reflecting back the light of our love toward the light of the moon that is her symbol." (lights large candle)

Leader (or other) says, "We are all made in the image of the Goddess. We are her children, no matter what our outward guise, and her light shines out from within us all. We light our own candles to honor both her and ourselves and to connect with the power of the full moon." (Each person lights their own candle. You can either do this together or go around the circle and do it in turn.)

Leader starts chant, and all join in: "I am the Goddess, and the Goddess is me." (Repeat for as long as it feels right, holding your candles up to the sky.)

Throw flower petals into the sky.

Take a moment or two to stand in silence and absorb the energy, then either blow out the candles or set them on the ground to burn as you pass cakes and ale (optional). If so, blow out the candles when you are done.

Leader (or other) says, "Our full moon rite is done. Well met by moonlight until we come together again. Blessed be."

All: "Blessed be!"

Full Moon Ritual 2

—water element—

There are many ways to celebrate the full moon if you have to be inside. One of the things you can do is make magical full moon water, which you can use in spells or rituals later on. This ritual can also be done outside if you are fortunate enough to be able to do so, but you don't need to be able to see the moon to feel its power.

Supplies: Small jars/glass containers with lids or stoppers (simple canning jars will work fine, although if you have something fancier, that's nice too). If your coven is the crafty sort, you can spend some time at the beginning of the ritual decorating the jars with glass paint or anything else that strikes your fancy. Small quartz crystals, one for each person (they can bring their own from home or the leader can provide them; the crystals should fit inside the containers you are using). A small bowl of sea salt. A pitcher of water, enough to at least partially fill each glass container. Purifying herbs or incense. Lengths of ribbon long enough to tie around the rim of each container (silver is nice, but any color will work, or you can have a variety and let people pick their own). Matches. Large Goddess candle. A table to act as an altar and hold all the working materials.

Optional: Background music such as drumming or chanting. Silver charms (moon shapes or pentacles are perfect, but anything silver will do, and they don't have to be large). Cakes and ale. Quarter candles. Glass paint, stencils, stickers, or anything else that can be used to decorate the glass containers. Notes for Goddess blessing.

To arrange the ritual: Place all the supplies on the table with the Goddess candle in the middle. If you are using quarter candles, they can either be put on the table at the proper directions (east, south, west, and north) or placed at the edges of the circle. If you can, set up where the moon can shine on you, but if that isn't possible, don't worry about it.

• • •

Gather in a circle around the altar table. Pass the purifying herbs or incense around to the left, taking as much time as you need for each person to waft it from head to toe. (If you are inside, these can be somewhat smoky and overwhelming. Be careful not to light too much of it.) The leader can say, "With this sacred smoke, we purify and cleanse ourselves for magical work, leaving the cares and worries of everyday life behind us."

Cast the circle hand to hand. The leader takes the hand of the person to their left and says, "We cast this circle hand to hand." Continue around the circle until all are holding hands and then say, "The circle is cast. We are between the worlds, in sacred space."

If you want, call the quarters, starting with east. Light candles for each direction in turn. Use a simple quarter call, such as: "We call to the east, the power of air, and ask you to join us in our circle." Repeat for all four directions.

Invoke the Goddess. The leader or some other member steps to the table and lights the Goddess candle, saying, "Great Lady of Light and Beauty, shine that light down upon us on this, your night of the full moon, and join us in our sacred circle as we gather together to celebrate you and all that is magical."

Each member takes a container. If you are decorating your glass containers, you can sit comfortably and do that now. Any symbols associated with the moon or the Goddess are appropriate, as are nature or magical images. When you are done, everyone should stand.

The leader holds the pitcher of water up toward the sky and says, "On this, the night of the full moon, we ask the Goddess to bless this water and fill it with her power so that we might use it for future magical work. So mote it be." The pitcher is handed around the circle, with each member holding it up and saying, "Bless this water, O Goddess." When it returns to the beginning, all say, "This water is blessed by the Goddess and the moon. So mote it be."

Each member (starting with the leader) steps to the table and pours some of the water from the pitcher into their individual containers. Then they sprinkle some of the sea salt into it, saying, "Salt water represents the ocean, whose tides are dictated by the pull of the moon. Salt water is in our blood and in our tears. We are the moon and the magic." (This can be written on a piece of paper on the table or given to each person individually to read if it is too long to memorize.)

Once each person has done this and returned to their places, each comes back to the table in turn (again, starting with the leader) and drops a crystal into their container and puts the top on. If using ribbons, they will then tie the ribbon around the top of the container, below the point where it closes (since you will want to be able to open the container in the future). You can use a simple knot or tie nine knots since that is a magical number. Each person says, "This crystal bears the essence of earth and the Goddess and the moon and magic. It too is blessed. And so my magical moon water is done and ready for future use. So mote it be." If using silver charms, add them to the ribbon now. Return to stand in the circle.

When all are finished, the leader holds their container up to the sky, and all others follow suit. The leader says, "We thank the Goddess for her gifts, for her power, and for her blessing; so mote it be."

All: "So mote it be."

Have cakes and ale (optional).

If you called the quarters, dismiss them in the reverse order you called them, starting in the north, saying something like, "North, power of earth, we thank you for your presence in our circle." (blow out candles)

Thank the Goddess. Leader says, "Thank you, Goddess, for your presence here in this circle tonight and in our lives always. Farewell and blessed be." (blow out candle)

Leader says, "The circle is open but never broken."

All: "Merry meet, merry part, and merry meet again!"

Full Moon Ritual

—just for two—

This ritual is best performed outside under the light of the moon, but if weather, space limitations, or privacy concerns mean that isn't possible, it is fine to do it inside. After all, the moon is still up there. While full moon rituals are wonderful to do under the shining orb after it has risen in the sky, general wisdom says it is okay to perform any ritual within two days before or after the actual date, and if you have to meet at seven and the moon doesn't rise until nine, it will make no difference at all in the energy of your magical work.

Full moon rituals usually focus on the Goddess since the lunar cycles are associated with her (the sabbats tend to include both the Goddess and the God). This is a simple ritual to connect with Goddess, nature, and each other.

Supplies: One white candle for each person (a votive or mini candle works well) plus one larger candle to represent the Goddess (white or silver or natural beeswax, which can always be substituted for any color). Purifying herbs or incense. Salt and water in two small bowls or already mixed together in one bowl. A table to use for an altar. Matches.

Optional: Drumming, rattles, chanting, or quiet background music. Food and drink for cakes and ale.

• • •

Sit or stand comfortably facing each other with your supplies laid out on an altar or table between you. Light the herbs or incense and take turns wafting it over each other from head to toe, focusing on cleansing and clearing away any stress or negativity from daily life. If you like, you can say, "With this sacred smoke, I clear and cleanse you to prepare for magical work."

Mix the salt and water together if you haven't already and anoint yourself at the points at your forehead, heart, and belly. (If you are very comfortable with the other person, you can do this for each other.) As you do so, say, "With salt and water, I clarify and clear my (your) mind, heart, and spirit to prepare for magical work."

Take a moment to center yourself, feeling the earth below and the sky above. If you can see the moon, you can gaze at her and blow her a kiss. Then do something with your magical partner to raise energy: this can be drumming or shaking rattles or repeating a simple chant (one of my favorites is "Fire am I, water am I, earth and air and spirit am I"). For something even simpler, you can join hands and hum together.

When you feel the moment is right, light your individual candles. Say, "I am one with the moon. I am one with the Goddess. I am magic and spirit." Then together light the Goddess candle off the wicks of your own candles. Take as long as you like to bask in the feeling of being in that full moon space.

When you're ready, thank the Goddess for her presence and snuff or blow out your individual candles. If it is safe to do so, you can leave the Goddess candle burning. If you want, share cakes and ale of some type, then one or both of you can say, "Our rite is done. We are back in the world."

Dark Moon Ritual

—clearing and cleansing to open the way—

One great way to maximize the magical potential of the lunar cycle is to practice at times other than the full moon. You may find that the energy feels different depending on the day and where you are in the cycle. It has been my experience that the full moon can feel buzzy and intense, while the dark moon is quieter and more subtle.

Blue Moon Circle likes to use dark moons, or new moons, for magical work that helps us with new beginnings or positive forward movement. Sometimes that's a spell for increasing prosperity or improving health issues. Sometimes we do clearing and cleansing work to remove anything that might be blocking our attempts to reach our goals.

Cleaning and cleansing magic is pretty basic and easy to do. If you happened to make full moon water (as described in the ritual before this), now would be a good time to use it. Otherwise you can bless and consecrate other water during this ritual.

Supplies: A bowl of water. A small bowl of sea salt. Purifying herbs or some cleansing incense (rosemary, sage, or lemon are good). Pieces of paper and pens. White or light blue votive candles in firesafe containers or on small plates (enough for everyone). A large white or silver candle for the Goddess. A table to use for an altar. Matches.

Optional: Drums or recorded drumming music. Four quarter candles (yellow, red, blue, and green or all white). A towel to dry wet hands on. Cakes and ale.

To arrange the ritual: Place everything on the altar table in the middle of the circle. If you are using quarter candles, they can either be put on the table at the proper directions (east, south, west, and north) or placed at the edges of the circle.

• • •

Pass herbs or incense around the circle, going to the left. You can do this in silence or the leader may say, "With this sacred smoke, we cleanse our bodies and spirits to prepare for the magical work we do tonight."

Cast the circle by the leader taking the hand of the person to their left and saying, "We cast this circle hand to hand." Continue around the circle until all are holding hands and then say, "The circle is cast. We are between the worlds in sacred space."

If you want, call the quarters, starting with east. Light candles for each direction in turn and use a simple quarter call, such as: "We call to the east, the power of air, and ask you to join us in our circle." Repeat for all four directions.

Invoke the Goddess. Leader or another member says, "Great Goddess, we call you to join us in our circle. Welcome and blessed be." Light the large candle.

Leader says, "Tonight is the new moon. It is a time for new beginnings and setting the stage for forward movement in the days ahead. But it can be hard to move forward when there are obstacles in our path that hold us back. Sometimes these come from the outside, but many times they come from within. Old habits we can't let go of, fear, self-limiting patterns we may not even be aware of—all these things can get in the way of us achieving what is important to us. Tonight we will do some magical cleansing and clearing, washing away anything negative that might impede our growth and success."

Pass out paper and pens. "Take a few moments to think about the things you know are getting in the way of whatever it is you want to achieve, whether they are from without or within. Visualize them clearly and then write them down on your paper. Take as long as you need." All write. If you are using recorded music, you can start it now. If people will be drumming, members can pick up their drums when they are done writing and provide background rhythm for those still thinking.

When everyone is done writing, the drumming should stop (recorded music can be left playing). Pass out the votive candles in their containers or on plates, but don't light them yet.

Leader or other member says, "Now that we have recognized some of the issues that stand in our way, we will cleanse ourselves with sacred water and wash them away." (If you are using full moon water that is already blessed, you can skip this next step.) Holds up bowl of water. "We ask the Goddess to bless and consecrate this water for magical use so that it may draw on the power of the moon to aid in our working." Place the water back on the edge of the altar table. "Each of us will approach the altar in turn and dip our fingers into the water, allowing it to pull out anything that no longer works for our benefit, and then anointing ourselves on the third eye (middle of the forehead), lips, heart, and belly. When you are done, return to your place in the circle and feel yourself growing lighter and lighter."

Each person takes a turn. When everyone is done, the leader or another member says, "Now it is time for the final step in our new moon ritual. Light the candle in front of you and put it on top of the list you wrote earlier. This symbolizes your willingness to let go of those issues. If you want, you can take your list home and safely burn it later."

All light their candles. The leader says, "Say after me: We release all that holds us back." All repeat. "We are cleansed and clear, ready to move forward without negativity or fear." All repeat. "The power of the Goddess and the moon lie within us, now and always." All repeat.

If drumming, spend a few minutes doing so. Otherwise, take a few moments of silence, then blow out the individual candles. Turn off recorded music if you used it.

Pass cakes and ale (optional).

If you called the quarters, dismiss them with a simple thanks. Blow out quarter candles.

Leader says, "Great Goddess, we thank you for your presence here in our circle, your aid and inspiration, and all the gifts you give us. Farewell and blessed be." Blow out Goddess candle.

All join hands and say, "The circle is open but never broken." Let go of hands.

section 7

the crafty coven

Not all witches enjoy crafting their own tools or making various magical items together, and that's okay. Not every witch is a crafty witch, and there are plenty of stores that sell cool premade goodies for the Pagan set. But if you like to create charm bags, poppets, rune stones and more, here are a few simple ideas for magical craft projects you can do as a group, with or without a ritual.

There are a few benefits to making your own magical supplies. For one thing, it is fun and a great way to bond as a group. But more importantly, when you craft something by hand, you put your own energy into it—your focus and your intention—and that can give whatever you are creating just that much more power when you actually use it. Also, did I mention that it is fun?

Blue Moon Circle has done many magical crafts together over the years. We've done knot magic, spun thread (two of us had spinning wheels, plus there were a couple of drop spindles), made corn dollies, sewn poppets, and made magical oils. One of the group was a potter for a while, and we used her clay and kiln to make our own rune stones. We decorated a group staff and then dedicated it. We even made our own magical candles on my stove. We are, it can be said, a pretty crafty group.

But you don't need any special talent or ability to do most magical crafts, which tend to be simple due to time constraints and the nature of Witchcraft itself. Even if you don't consider yourself particularly creative, it is worth trying a few projects as a coven.

Once you have finished crafting whatever it is you are making, you may want to bless and consecrate it for positive magical work. Obviously, you have already put lots of good energy into whatever it is, but this step makes it official, as it were. The same basic spell can be used for nearly everything you make in circle (or on your own), and it adds an extra little bit of power and spark.

A General Blessing and Consecrating Spell

This step is usually done when you have finished making the item but before you use it. If you are crafting something that will be utilized later on in the ritual in which it was created, you can do the blessing and consecrating as part of the flow of the ritual or skip it if you choose.

There is no wrong way to do this. This particular example is the process by which Blue Moon Circle usually blesses and consecrates things, but there are plenty of other approaches, and you should do whatever feels right to you. Some people use a drop of their own blood. Others prefer to leave their new tools out under the full moon. You can do any or all of these or a combination. The following is just the simplest approach. Each person can do their own tool separately or in unison, or you can take turns blessing all the items (for instance, one member calls on the blessing of air for everyone).

Supplies: Something to represent each of the four elements, usually a candle for fire, purifying herbs or incense for air (because of the smoke, although you can also use a feather), salt for earth (or a rock or crystal or sand), and water for, um, water. Something to represent either the Goddess or the Goddess and the God, usually a candle or a statue, but you can also simply call on them if you prefer. Some people use the herbs/incense to represent both fire and air and mix salt and water for earth and water.

Optional: Altar table or cloth.

• • •

Place the newly created (or newly purchased or gifted) magical item on an altar table or cloth, or hold it in your hand.

Say, "I bless this ________ with the power of air." Waft the purifying herbs or incense over it or wave the feather if using that. You can also blow a gentle breath over the item instead.

Say, "I bless this ________ with the power of water." Sprinkle a few drops of water over it from the tips of your fingers. Be careful if the item is something that could be damaged from too much water. You can also simply wet the tip of a finger with your own saliva or a tear.

Say, "I bless this ________ with the power of earth." Sprinkle some salt over the item, or a bit of sand, or pass a crystal over the top, perhaps stopping to rest it gently for a minute.

Say, "I bless this ________ with the power of fire." Pass a lit candle carefully over the item. If you are outside and have a bonfire, you can (even more carefully) hold the item near the flames. If you are doing this outside during the day, the light of the sun can be substituted for an actual flame.

Say, "I ask the Goddess and God to bless this ________, and I pledge to use it well." If you are using candles to represent the gods, pick up the item and pass it carefully over them. Otherwise you can simply hold it up toward the sky.

Say, "This ________ has been blessed and consecrated for positive magical work. May it serve me well from this day forward. So mote it be."

SECTION 7

General Ritual Notes and Suggestions for Doing Crafts in Sacred Space

There are a couple of different ways you can go about doing craft work in sacred space, and you can either choose one or the other every time you do this type of work or decide on a case-by-case basis what feels right.

The first approach is to do your crafting within a full-on ritual format: cast the circle, call the quarters, invoke the Goddess (or God), and so on. The other alternative is to keep things simple and merely cast the circle (or do whatever it is you do to establish you are in sacred space—for Blue Moon Circle, after our many years of practice together, this may be as basic as passing the sage wand and concentrating on being in circle together). If you are not doing major spellwork, there may be no need to go through all the formal steps of ritual. On the other hand, if it helps you and your coven focus and feel that your craft, whatever it might be, is more powerful and magical, by all means do the whole shebang.

You can try it one way, and if it doesn't feel right, try it the other way. In my experience, most magical craft projects are fun and creative, and although you are channeling magical energy into the work, don't necessarily require a formal ritual format to accomplish your goals. This is a decision you can discuss as a coven. Just remember to enjoy the process, whichever approach you take.

In the projects that follow, I will leave out the more ceremonial aspects. Feel free to use them, following examples from earlier in the book, if you so choose, or any variation that feels right to you. Unlike many rituals where it is best to keep chatter to a minimum, during crafting circles you can decide if you want to work in silence or talk about what it is you are doing.

Magical Candles

Candles are one of the easiest and most commonly used tools. For much of my solitary spell work, I simply light a candle and speak to the gods or recite whichever spell I feel is best for the moment. They have the added advantage of being innocuous—plenty of non-witchy people have candles around their houses, after all. Nothing to see here.

But there are ways to take the basic candle and lift it to another level, magically speaking. If you want to get really serious about it, you can make your own. It's not difficult, as long as you have the right supplies, and Blue Moon Circle used to make our own magical candles from scratch, melting the wax on my stove, adding specific essential oils, the colors we wanted, and more. If you are so inclined, it can be a lot of fun, and you can imbue a surprising amount of power into anything you create from start to finish. It is messy, and if one of your group doesn't already have the right supplies (I did, at the time), it can get expensive.

The next best thing is to take a premade candle and make it magical by adding your own personal touches. This is actually quite easy and can be done either as part of a larger ritual (say, prosperity work) or as its own crafty endeavor. Once you are done creating your candles, you may want to bless and consecrate them for future magical work using the previous ritual.

Supplies: Candles (these can be tapers or votives in any color you choose, although be aware that it can be hard to see symbols carved into white wax). Toothpicks or some other tool for carving (people can carefully use their athames or any other pointed item). Essential oils or magical oils that have been created already or purchased (which oils you use will vary depending on the intended purpose of the candles and whether or not you are crafting them for a specific use).

Optional: Colored ribbons to tie around the base of the candles (for instance, green for prosperity, pink for love, blue for healing, etc.).

Herbs to roll the candles in (again, these will vary depending on the purpose, and you may want to use them sparsely or only at the very bottom edge of the candle since they can be flammable). White glue or a lighter. Paper plates or waxed paper. Printed handouts with runes or other symbols if people aren't familiar with the ones you will be using.

If you are planning to anoint your candles with essential oils (as opposed to premade magical oils with a specific intent, such as healing or protection), here are a few simple correspondences you may want to follow. If using essential oils, it is best to put them into some kind of carrier oil, such as almond, coconut, or olive, to dilute them. If you want to make a candle for more general use, choose a couple oils that seem the most powerful to you and smell pleasant when combined, and use those. You can also use this list for dried herbs. You can see from the following brief list of more commonly used herbs that many of them are good for more than one thing. If you're not sure what you're going to be using the candle for in the future, you may want to pick a couple of the multipurpose herbs.

Healing—Chamomile, lavender, eucalyptus, dill, geranium, lemon balm, peppermint, rose, rosemary, thyme

Love—Rose, lavender, chamomile, basil, cinnamon, clove, geranium, lemon, lemon balm, thyme

Prosperity—Basil, cinnamon, clove, dill, ginger, patchouli, peppermint, sandalwood

Protection—Basil, chamomile, dill, cinnamon, eucalyptus, geranium, garlic, parsley, juniper, rose, rosemary, sage

Place all the supplies on a table and get comfortable. You don't need to use an altar table if you aren't doing this in formal ritual space, and it can sometimes be easier to simply sit around a regular kitchen or dining room table, although Blue Moon Circle usually uses our altar table because it is round.

• • •

If you are casting a circle, calling the quarters, and so on, do that now.

Each coven member should take a candle and a carving tool if they haven't brought their own. You can decide as a group to all make candles with the same purpose or to each make your own type of candle to fit your individual needs.

Start by carving runes or other symbols into the side of your candle with the toothpick or other tool. Focus on your intention and put your energy into the candle as you work. You aren't limited to runes. You can carve your initials, your magical name if you have one, any symbols associated with magic (such as a pentacle, a sun, a crescent moon, and so on) or symbols associated with the specific purpose of your candle if there is one (such as a dollar sign for prosperity, a caduceus for healing, a snake for transformation, or anything else that feels right to you).

Now you can anoint your candles with whichever oils you are using. This is done by putting a drop of oil on your fingertip and rubbing it onto the candle upward from the bottom. Be careful not to get any on the wick since many oils are flammable.

If you are using dried herbs, you can either smooth a bit of white glue over the candle or use a lighter or matches to slightly soften the wax so the herbs will stick. Keep in mind that you don't actually want to melt the candle. Then place the herbs onto a paper plate or a piece of paper and roll the candle until you have the amount of herbs you desire on the sides.

If you want, finish it off by tying a ribbon around the bottom of the candle. For an extra magical touch, tie the ribbon using nine knots since nine is a sacred magical number.

Bless and consecrate if desired.

Poppets

Poppets are a form of sympathetic magic that has been used in many cultures across the world. They are essentially a human figure—usually a very basic two legs, two arms, and a head—which is then decorated to reflect the person it is supposed to represent. While they can be made out of anything, clay or fabric are the most commonly used materials.

While it is certainly possible to perform spells on a poppet that is intended to stand for someone else, most modern eclectic witches prefer to make poppets that represent themselves since that doesn't interfere with free will. The one exception to this is healing work that is done with the permission of the person for whom it is performed.

Cloth poppets, or dollies, are easy to make and tend to use materials most of us have around the house. They are also fairly innocuous looking, and you can place a piece of paper inside on which you have written your magical goal or whatever spell you are using. If you wish to reuse your poppet, you can even take out a few stitches and replace your old goal with a new one.

Supplies: A piece of fabric (natural fabrics such as cotton are best, and you may wish to stick to neutral light colors, which are easy to draw on). The fabric should be about twice as long as it is wide, so you can use a piece that is 4 inches wide and 8 inches long, although you can make your poppet as large or small as you choose. Thread. Needle. Scissors. Something to stuff the poppet with (cotton balls, tissues, pillow stuffing, etc.). Markers. Small piece of paper. Pen.

Optional: Yarn for hair. Herbs to put inside. Beads or any other decorative items.

• • •

Double the fabric over so that it is a square piece with the fold at the top, where the head will be. You can cut the entire poppet out, but if you leave the fold at the top there will be less sewing. Draw your figure on the cloth with a marker and cut out your doll.

You then start sewing it together. If you left the fold at the head, start on one side where the fabric is cut; otherwise, you can start anywhere. Just remember to leave a large-enough opening to get the stuffing inside. Don't worry if you are not the world's neatest seamstress. This isn't a work of art; it is magic. With every stitch you make, concentrate on the purpose of your poppet and who it is supposed to represent.

Once you have it mostly sewn, poke your stuffing inside. Alternately, you can stuff it as you go. If you are using them, add herbs at this point to boost your work. (For instance, if you are doing a poppet for healing, you might want to add dried calendula and lavender.)

Then take your piece of paper and pen and write down either your magical goal (prosperity, healing, focus and concentration, good sleep, whatever it is) or any spell you've chosen to use. Tuck it inside and finish sewing the poppet shut.

Decorate your poppet as desired. Draw eyes, nose, and mouth. You can add yarn for hair or draw it on. You can add designs by sewing on beads. For instance, if you are doing love magic, you can sew on beads in the shape of a heart on the poppet's chest. If you are doing healing work, you can place beads on any spot that needs special attention. If the poppet represents you, add anything you think makes it more personal.

When you are done, you can bless and consecrate it. Put it someplace safe: your altar, under your pillow, or in a drawer or box. If you have made a very small poppet, you might even want to wear it in a pouch around your neck. When you are done with it, disassemble it carefully and with respect, and thank it for the work it did for you.

Books of Shadows

You could say I am something of an expert on Books of Shadows. After all, I literally wrote a book called *The Eclectic Witch's Book of Shadows: Witchy Wisdom at Your Fingertips*. But really, it doesn't take a lot of know-how to create one for either yourself or for your coven.

A Book of Shadows is the modern name (probably invented by Gerald Gardner in the 1940s) for a grimoire, or a book of magic. There are no specific instructions for creating one since each witch's book is different. Wiccan covens usually had a Book of Shadows that belonged to the coven, and those who joined were allowed to copy the information it held, as long as they pledged to keep it secret.

A Book of Shadows is basically a place to write down your magical knowledge, as well as any other information you consider important to your magical practice. For an individual, this may include information on stones, herbs, divination, a record of meaningful dreams, messages from the gods, and even recipes. For a coven, it is more likely to be a compilation of the work you have done together.

Blue Moon Circle started a Book of Shadows for the group when we first began. It included the spell we used to bless the book, the signed names of all who belonged at the time, and a copy of the Charge of the Goddess (a famous Wiccan text often recited on the night of the full moon). Over the many years of our practice, we have added all the spells and rituals we have done together, any information we discussed during the rituals (such as the aforementioned stones and herbs), and even pictures of the group when we were gathered together.

For us, it is not only a magical tool but also a record of our journey together as a coven; it's priceless. If you decide to create a Book of Shadows for your own coven, there are a few things to figure out before you start:

- What kind of book do you want? Large or small? Premade or crafted by hand?
- What do you want to put into it? Magical information people have gathered? Only things done together as a group? Rituals and spells?
- Who gets to hold on to it? Does it stay at one person's house or move from place to place?
- Is it okay for members to share the information in it with others or is it a secret?

Once you have these details figured out, it is a simple enough matter to create a Book of Shadows that is perfect for your own particular coven. The instructions below are just one approach, and you can change them up to suit your own needs and group style. Suitable blank books can be found at most Pagan shops, some bookstores, and online. If you have an artsy group, you can get one with a blank cover and decorate it yourselves. Otherwise you can buy one that has a witchy cover; the one Blue Moon Circle uses is a large black book with a gold pentacle on the front.

Supplies: Large blank book. Markers (they even make ones that mimic calligraphy for those who want to make it look as though the writing is fancy without actually learning that particular skill). Each member should bring something to contribute to the book that they feel is meaningful or important: a poem, magical information, witchy wisdom they found in a favorite book—these can be handwritten or printed on paper. Clear tape or glue. Supplies to bless and consecrate the book as noted earlier in this section: something to represent each of the four elements, usually a candle for fire, herbs or incense or a feather for air, salt for earth (or a rock or crystal or sand), and a bowl of water. A candle for the Goddess and one for the God, if using.

Optional: A cloth to lay the book on while you are blessing it and possibly to keep it wrapped up in later if you choose. Art supplies if you will be decorating the book, such as paint, pens, colorful markers, glitter and glue, glitter pens, stickers, stamps, etc.

• • •

Arrange the supplies on a table or a cloth on the floor you can comfortably gather around.

On the inside of the book, everyone can write their name (full name or first name or a magical name if they have one). Use a marker or different-colored markers for each person and your nicest handwriting. You can add the date if you want.

Each person should explain what their contribution to the book is and why it is important or meaningful. Then they can tape or glue it onto one of the blank pages (or copy it in by hand if they have good penmanship). You may want to discuss them all first and then decide if there is a particular order you want them to go into the book.

If you are decorating the outside of the book (or the inside of the front or back covers), take turns passing the book around the table so each person can add their individual touches. If necessary, the book can go around more than once.

When the book is complete, bless and consecrate it, and dedicate it to positive magical work. If you wish, you can use this blessing that Blue Moon Circle put inside our own book and that was printed in *The Eclectic Witch's Book of Shadows*. Recite it together with your hands held over the book.

Bless this book
In the name of the God and the Goddess
Who guide my feet on the Path of Beauty
Let it be filled with wisdom and knowledge
Let me use it only for good
Let me share it with those who need it
Let it help me grow in my craft
And in my life
So mote it be!

Creating a Group Staff

Creating a group staff is much like creating a group Book of Shadows or any other coven tool. Each person should contribute something that has meaning to them and share in the decorating of the staff. You simply use different adornments. The staff itself can be obtained in any number of ways. You can buy one, of course, or use one that a member of the coven already has. Or you can search the nearby woods (if you are lucky enough to have some) for the perfect stick. It should be about shoulder height (four and a half or five feet, although there is no specific "right" height) and sturdy without being too heavy to pass around a ritual circle. I have lots of trees on my property, so I was able to find a perfect branch just lying around.

Ask people ahead of time to bring an item or items to add to the staff. These can be anything from feathers to beads to small magical charms or figures. Keep in mind that they will have to be attached to the staff somehow (usually with wire, thread, or leather thong) so it helps if they have a hole or can be wrapped (like the top of a feather). A staff is handled too much to make gluing a very good option.

As with all other magical tools you craft as a group, you may wish to bless and consecrate the staff when you are done, using the instructions and supplies listed earlier in this chapter.

Supplies: A tall, reasonably straight piece of wood to use as the staff. Lengths of different colored ribbon. String, thread, thin flexible wire, or thin leather cord. Various decorations such as feathers, beads, crystals, charms, etc. Fine point markers.

Optional: Wood-burning tool (if one of your members happens to have one).

• • •

Arrange all the materials on a table or cloth and sit comfortably around it.

Each person should choose a marker and a length of ribbon in a color that appeals to them. They can write or draw anything they want on the ribbon, remembering that the energy they put into what they are doing will become a permanent part of the staff. When Blue Moon Circle did this, we each wrote down things we liked or admired about the other members of the coven or the group as a whole, but you can also just put your names, magical symbols, or even short spells or prayers.

When everyone is finished, take turns tying your ribbons near the top of the staff. If you want, you can fasten them all together first with thread or wire and then bind them on as one piece.

Pass the staff around the circle so that everyone gets a chance to add the token they brought plus any other decorations they want. They can also write in marker on the wood itself or use the wood-burning tool (if you happen to have one) to add symbols or their initials.

This should be a joyous activity, so remember to have fun. When the staff is complete, you can bless and consecrate it if you want to. It can either stay at the leader's house (or wherever it is you meet to practice the most often, if it is someone else's home) or spend some time with each person in the coven.

Charm Bags and Sachets

Charm bags and sachets are useful magical tools that are both simple and fun to make. They don't require exotic ingredients and can usually be created out of items you already have, especially if you are the type of witch who keeps a basic supply of herbs, stones, and other magical ingredients around. (Hint: You probably should do this if you can.)

Charm bags and sachets are essentially the same thing—the only difference is that charm bags have an opening at the top that ties or pulls shut, and sachets are little pillows that are sewn shut. Charm bags can be worn around the neck on a string or chain, but usually both are either tucked into a pocket or purse, underneath a pillow, or placed on an altar. I have a protection charm bag that hangs by the front door of my house, for instance.

These types of magical crafts are usually created for a specific purpose, such as protection, prosperity, healing, or love. Which ingredients you use will vary depending on what that purpose is, so you should discuss it within the coven (possibly at the meeting before this craft is done or else by communicating beforehand) and choose a focus. Either that or the leader can simply pick one they think will appeal to everyone taking part.

Supplies: Small muslin, velveteen, or cotton drawstring bags—**OR**—pieces of cloth about 3 inches long by 6 inches wide (these can be larger if you want to fit more inside) and needles and thread to sew them with. If you'd rather not sew, you can cut a square piece of cloth and use a ribbon or a piece of yarn to tie it shut instead. Depending on the goal of the work, various herbs and tumbled stones or crystals, one for each bag.

NOTE: You can choose the color of your bags to fit the magical work you will be doing, such as blue for healing, green for prosperity, and white or black for protection, or simply use a neutral color.

Optional: Magical oil for anointing. Any other ingredients that seem appropriate for the goal you are working on. You can write the magical intention on a piece of paper and stick it inside or use markers or fabric paint to draw something on the fabric (a heart for love magic, for instance, or dollar signs for prosperity work). You can put in a coin for prosperity, working on the "like draws like" principle. The only limit is your imagination.

• • •

Place your magical supplies on a table and sit comfortably around it.

Spend a little time discussing the magical goal and what it means to each of you. Remind people to focus on their intention during the preparation of the bags/sachets. If you are sewing, think about your goal with every stitch. Think about it as you add each ingredient.

If you will be making your bag or sachet, either sew up both sides, leaving one end open and placing the herbs, stone, and anything else inside, then either wrap a ribbon around the end or sew it shut. If making a bundle without sewing, lay the cloth flat, place the herbs and such inside, then gather the edges together and tie a ribbon or string around it. Of course, if you are using a premade bag, simply place the ingredients inside. Just remember to do this slowly and mindfully.

When you are done, you can anoint the charm bag with magical oil (optional).

If desired, you can then bless and consecrate the bag or sachet, using the instructions at the beginning of the chapter.

Herb or Stone Exchange

Some covens (Blue Moon Circle included) like to do the occasional ritual that is both practical and informative, rather than only focusing on the magical (not that there is anything wrong with that). Over the years we have done a number of rituals where different members took turns coming up with an idea for a theme. The herb exchange was one of these.

"Ritual" is probably not really the right word for these gatherings, although they still take place in circle, usually on full moons or occasionally on a sabbat that seems appropriate for the topic. You could do an herb exchange on Lammas or Mabon, for instance, since they are harvest festivals. I think we did this one on the summer solstice, since midsummer is a traditional time to harvest herbs, especially those used in magical work.

We often cast the circle, called the quarters, and invoked the God and Goddess as we would usually do, but that isn't strictly necessary when you are doing these kinds of non-magical activities. You can simply sit in a circle in your sacred space, maybe passing the purifying herbs or incense first to remind your subconscious that you are doing spiritual work.

The herb exchange is simple, fun, and educational—plus, you get to take things home when it is over! Each member brings an herb they like in small individual pots (we have a lot of gardeners in our group, but not everyone grows herbs, and it is fine to go out and buy yours), enough for each member to have one. It is a good idea to coordinate who is bringing what ahead of time so you don't end up with six people all bringing peppermint.

Along with the plants, each person should bring a slip of paper on which they have written (or typed) the magical information associated with the herb they've chosen. For instance, if someone brings lavender, they may have a paper that says something like this:

> Lavender is used magically for peace, sleep, healing, and love. It also has medicinal uses, including insomnia and the treatment of bug bites and burns. It's edible and is sometimes put into baked goods.

Each member of the coven presents their herb and explains its properties, and then gives out the extras to the others so they can smell it, look at it, and eventually take it home. One of the great things about this kind of group work is that each person only has to research one plant, and yet you end up learning about—and having a sample of—as many different herbs as there are people in your group. Fun, educational, and practical.

If you want, you can do some form of magical work at the end using a bit of each plant in some kind of spell or blessing and consecrating all the herbs for magical use. Blue Moon Circle mostly just had fun sharing the information and the plants, and felt that the regular ritual elements at the beginning and the end were enough for us. There's no wrong way.

This kind of sharing ritual also can be done with gemstones, where you can use small tumbled stones that are inexpensive enough to manage one for each person in the group. Sharing knowledge and learning from each other is one of the benefits of being in a coven, and this is a great example of how you can do that within a circle setting, although if you choose to be less formal, there is no reason you can't do this sort of thing just hanging out inside someone's living room or out in the yard.

If you have individual or group Books of Shadows, you can write the information down in those for future reference or bring copies of the information to share with everyone, so you each go home with not just a selection of plants or rocks, but also the magical knowledge that goes with each one.

NOTE: People should make sure that any plants they bring are pet-safe if there are members of the coven who have animal companions who might be able to get at them. For instance, lilies are extremely poisonous to cats, so that might be added to the shared information.

Section 8

Rituals with a Purpose

One of the benefits of practicing with a coven is that you can do magical work for a specific purpose with the energetic boost that comes from working together with others for the benefit of all. While solitary witches can absolutely generate powerful magic all on their own, work done with others has its particular charm (you should excuse the pun).

There is no limit to the kind of magical work you can do within a coven setting. The examples I have here are some of the more common types, but Blue Moon Circle has done everything from magic to assure one of our members had the best possible surgical outcome to spells for easing the grief of losing a loved one. Whatever a member of your coven needs, you can undoubtedly come up with a ritual that will help, although usually rituals are more general and address issues that touch everyone in one way or another.

All these rituals work well on the full moon, but you can do them whenever they are needed. Depending on your coven's wishes, you may choose to do a full circle casting, quarter calls, and Goddess invocation (you can invoke the God too, but if you are spellcasting on the full moon, you will probably just invoke the Goddess). If so, you can follow the directions in section 2, examples from earlier rituals in the book, or create your own variations.

Whether or not you go with the complete formal ritual format, you will probably want to do something to signify that you have entered sacred space, whether that means passing purifying herbs or by casting the circle hand to hand or having the leader say, "We are in sacred space outside the world, safe and protected." It is always a good idea to reinforce the feeling of being in circle and remind people to focus on the magical instead of the mundane.

Healing

Healing can mean a lot of different things. There is the obvious physical healing from illness or injury, of course, but there is also mental and spiritual healing. This healing ritual can be used for any or all of these, even healing relationships or, if your coven is truly ambitious, the planet. Your group may wish to focus their intentions on one particular type of healing or each person can focus on the kind of healing they need the most.

Supplies: Blue candles on firesafe plates (one for each person). Healing herbs (any combination of chamomile, dill, eucalyptus, lavender, lemon balm, peppermint, rose petals or rose hips, rosemary, and thyme; you should probably use at least three of these, either dried or fresh will do, and if you want, you can ask each member to bring a different herb to share). Handouts with the spell and symbols for the following runes: Kenaz, Uruz, Sigel, Tir, and Ing (if you want to go that extra step, you can look up their associations with healing and put that on the papers too). Large white candle for the Goddess. Sea salt and water in separate containers and a small bowl to mix them in. Table to use as an altar. Purifying herbs or any healing incense (see herbs above). Matches. Toothpicks.

Optional: Quarter candles. Small quartz crystals. Cakes and ale.

Note: If you wish to call on a specific goddess who is associated with healing, you may want to consider Brigid, Isis, Kuan Yin, or Rhiannon.

To arrange the ritual: Each person should be given a blue candle, a toothpick, and a quartz crystal (optional), as well as the paper with the spell and rune symbols. All the other supplies can be arranged neatly on the altar table, with the Goddess candle in the middle and the herbs/incense, salt, and water in front of the ritual leader.

• • •

Gather in a circle around the altar table. Pass the purifying herbs or incense around the circle. The leader can say, "With this sacred smoke, we purify and cleanse ourselves and our circle and prepare ourselves to do magical work."

The leader or someone else mixes the salt and water together in the bowl and says, "With salt and water, we cleanse and purify our bodies and spirits, preparing for the work that lies ahead." They dip their fingers into the mixture and touch it to forehead (third eye), lips, heart, and core (stomach), then pass it to the next person in the circle.

Cast the circle from hand to hand or by having the leader say, "The circle is cast; we are between the worlds in sacred space."

If calling quarters and doing a formal Goddess invocation, do that now.

Leader says, "We have come together tonight to work on healing. All of us have areas in our lives that could use some healing magic. These might be physical or mental or spiritual. Perhaps it is our relationships with others or the earth we hold so dear that needs to be healed. Take a moment to think about where you wish to send healing energy. When you're ready, pick up your candle and use the toothpick to carve whatever seems appropriate into the surface. There are runes associated with healing on the paper you were given. You can also write your name, words that represent the issue or issues you wish to heal, or anything else that seems right to you. Remember that you can't heal anyone else, only yourself, although you can always send good energy toward those you care about."

Take some time for people to do this. Wait until everyone is done. As people are waiting, they can focus on their intentions and whatever it is they wish to heal.

Once everyone is done, pass the healing herbs around the circle, one at a time. Name each one as it is passed and explain that these herbs are associated with healing. Instruct circle members to sprinkle some of each herb onto the plate that holds their candle.

If using crystals, tell people to place their crystal onto the plate as well. Explain that crystal quartz has long been associated with healing as well as the power of the Goddess and the moon.

Light the Goddess candle in the middle of the table and say, "Goddess (or specific name), we ask that you send us healing. Help us mend what is broken, bring light where there is darkness, and transform stagnation and negativity into positive change and growth. We light these candles to signify our willingness to embrace that positive change."

Have each person step forward, one at a time, and light their blue candle off the flame on the Goddess candle, being careful not to disturb the herbs or stones on their plates, and then step back into their spot in the circle.

When everyone's candle is lit, say the spell together.

Let what is sick be well
Let what is broken be healed

Let what is filled with sorrow be replaced by joy
Let all things be as they should be
Healed with the power of magic
and the will of the Goddess
All shall be well, all shall be well, and
all manner of things shall be well
So mote it be!

Stand in silence for a few moments.

If you are including cakes and ale, pass them now.

When the ritual is over, the candles can be blown out and taken home so that people can continue to light them daily or as needed.

If you called the quarters, dismiss them now.

If you invoked the Goddess, you can thank her now.

Open the circle by joining hands and then letting go, saying, "The circle is open but never broken. Merry meet, merry part, and merry meet again!"

Prosperity

Prosperity can mean different things to different people, especially depending on the circumstances they happen to be dealing with at the time. Most people think of money when they do prosperity work, and certainly there is nothing wrong with doing magical work when you need help with your general financial situation.

On the other hand, sometimes what you need has less to do with cash and more to do with getting the perfect new job or finding the right house at a price you can afford or getting rid of debt. So when you are doing prosperity workings, it may be a good idea to keep your options open rather than asking for one specific thing. Sometimes the gods surprise you by sending prosperity in a form you might not have thought of.

Another thing to consider is how that prosperity comes about. For instance, you don't want to suddenly have lots of money because someone you love dies and leaves it to you, and you don't want to acquire newfound prosperity if someone else is going to suffer because of it. I tend to be a bit cautious when it comes to prosperity work and often add the phrase "For the good of all and according to the free will of all" at the end of those kinds of spells, just to make my intentions clear to the universe.

There are those who believe that Witchcraft shouldn't be used for prosperity work at all, as if benefiting from magical work is somehow cheating or in bad taste. I think that's pretty silly. After all, it never hurts to ask for something. If the gods don't want us to have it, they won't give it to us. There is nothing wrong with using all the tools you have to improve your life, including Witchcraft.

This is a simple spell to create a magical talisman that will draw prosperity to you in whichever way is best for you at the moment. Once it is created, you can place it on your altar or under your pillow, carry it around in your pocket, or wear it around your neck in a small bag, wallet, or purse.

Supplies: A fancy coin for each person (this can be a half dollar or dollar coin, a foreign or antique coin that looks cool to you, or even a brand-new very shiny penny, although I like to go with the bigger coins because they have a special feel to me; each person can bring their own or the ritual leader can provide them). Magical prosperity oil (you can buy or make this out of some of the following essential oils) or essential oil of basil, cinnamon, clove, patchouli, peppermint, or sandalwood. Purifying herbs or incense. Green or white candle. A small bowl of salt. A small bowl of water. A table to use as an altar or a cloth to spread on the ground. Copies of the spell for each participant. Matches.

Optional: Small drawstring bags to put the coins in when you're done.

To arrange the ritual: Put all supplies on an altar table or on the floor or ground on a cloth and sit comfortably around it. Hand around the coins if people haven't brought their own.

• • •

Light the purifying herbs / incense and pass it around the circle to the left. Leader can say, "With this blessed smoke, we waft away all the negativity of our daily lives and enter into sacred space clean and clear and ready for magical work."

If desired, do a formal circle casting, call the quarters, and invoke the Goddess and God.

Leader can discuss the points about prosperity discussed earlier or people can talk about what kinds of prosperity they need in their lives right now or both.

Pass the magical oil or oils around the table. Each person should put a dab of oil on the tip of a finger and lightly draw the rune symbol Gifu, which looks like an X, on their coin. This is a way of asking the gods for their gifts, whatever they might be.

The leader says, "We bless and consecrate this talisman for prosperity with the power of water." Pass the bowl of water around the table. Each person should sprinkle a little bit on top of their coin.

The leader or someone else says, "We bless and consecrate this talisman for prosperity with the power of air." Light the purifying herbs or incense and pass around the table for everyone to waft smoke over their coin.

The leader or someone else says, "We bless and consecrate this talisman for prosperity with the power of earth." Pass the bowl of salt and have each person sprinkle a little over their coin.

The leader or someone else says, "We bless and consecrate this talisman for prosperity with the power of fire." Light the green or white candle in the middle of the table and have each person carefully hold their coin over it, far enough away that they don't get burned.

Leader says, "Our talismans are almost ready. Now we will recite this spell to activate the magic we have imbued them with and the intent we have put into them for any and all positive forms of prosperity."

God and Goddess, bless these coins
That they may be the symbols of our magic
And our faith in the universe
That they may bring us prosperity
in the best possible ways
For whatever our needs might be
For the good of all and
according to the free will of all
Bless these talismans
So mote it be!

If using small bags or pouches, coins can be put in them now.

If you did a formal circle casting and the rest, dismiss the quarters and open the circle.

Protection

Protection work is one of the mainstays of Witchcraft. This is one of the few areas where it is okay to do magical work for others, like your children or your friends, although it is always best to ask permission first since not everyone is comfortable having magic done on their behalf. Which of us couldn't use a little more protection? It is a scary world out there.

And it always has been. Historically, witches have woven protection magic into their family's clothing and done protection magic on crops and animals and, of course, on themselves. Whether you are dealing with a particularly difficult situation or just trying to keep yourself safe in general, a little bit of protection magic is never a bad idea.

I do protection work on my house and property every year in the fall as I prepare for winter and the challenges that come with it. I make up a simple herbal mixture combined with sea salt and sprinkle it around the outside of the house (it's a bit messy for inside, although you can use it indoors if you don't mind vacuuming up after yourself once it has had a chance to settle in) and the edges of my property where it meets the road. That includes the mailbox, since a lot of things come into the house through there.

This ritual is a variation on that. You can either take the herbal mixture and use it around your home or you can place it into a charm bag and hang it up near the entrance or wherever feels right to you. If you can't have it out in the open, you can put it in the drawer of a table near the door or even bury it under a doormat or inside a window box, in which case you may wish to enclose the charm bag in something that will keep it dry.

One of the benefits of doing protection magic as a group is that the energy of everyone involved goes into the work and magnifies the protective power for all.

Supplies: Small jars or bags to put the herbal mix into. Dried herbs in individual bowls or containers (basil, chamomile, cinnamon, dill, garlic, parsley, rosemary, sage—you can use four or five of these, and leave out the garlic if you are going to use the mixture inside). Coarse salt. Copies of the spell for everyone. Purifying herbs or incense. Table to use as an altar. Matches.

Optional: A tumbled gemstone for each person (black onyx or red jasper are good choices). Salt. Water. Black or white candle if you plan on blessing and consecrating the herbal mixture once it is made.

To arrange the ritual: Place all the herbs and anything else you're using on the table. Pass out jars or bags and a copy of the spell to each participant.

• • •

Pass the purifying herbs/incense around the table. Each person can waft the smoke over themselves and also toward the supplies on the altar table. Leader can say, "With this blessed smoke, we waft away all the negativity of our daily lives and enter into sacred space clean and clear and ready for magical work."

If desired, you can do a formal circle casting now, call the quarters, and invoke the Goddess and God.

Leader can talk about the traditional use of protection work by witches. If you want, everyone can discuss the areas in their lives where they feel vulnerable or things and people they would like to protect.

Everyone should take some of each herb and put it into their container. You can either pass the bowls around the table or have people take turns coming up to the table, whichever works best for the amount of participants you have. This should be done quietly and mindfully, keeping the intention of protection in focus. If you are using the stone, it can be added now.

Once everyone has their protection mix, you can say the spell together.

With these herbs, gifts of the gods and the earth,
I protect all that is dear to me
With my craft, gift of the gods and the universe,
I protect all that I value
With this spell, spoken amongst friends,

I protect what is mine from any harm, intentional or accidental
This magic will bring protection
So mote it be!

If you wish to bless and consecrate your protection mixture, you can do so now, using the directions from earlier in this section.

If you called the quarters and invoked the Goddess, dismiss the quarters now and thank the Goddess.

To open the circle, you can say, "Merry meet, merry part, and merry meet again."

Love

When most people think about doing love magic, the first thing that springs to mind is romantic love. But while that can be wonderful, there are also many other kinds of love in our lives, any of which we might wish to increase, improve, or call into being. There is the love of family, true and lasting friendship, and the love we have for our beloved animal companions, among others.

I am not a big fan of the traditional love spell. Most of the ones you see come dangerously close to interfering with free will, and it is all too easy to cast a spell that will backfire and end up creating a magical connection between you and someone you later want to get away from, only to discover it isn't that easy.

Instead, I suggest casting a spell that will give the gods and the universe the opportunity to send you the kind of love you most need in that particular moment, whether or not you know it. Of course, you too have free will, and if you wish to cast this spell with the intention to bring you romantic love, that's just fine. As long as you leave it open-ended (so if the person you are so sure you are supposed to be with isn't, in fact, meant for you), the door is still open for the right one to find you.

Supplies: Pink or white candles on a firesafe plate for each person. A piece of tumbled or crystal rose quartz or amethyst for each person. Rose petals or lavender. Copies of the spell. Pieces of paper and pens. An assortment of pink and red ribbons cut to fit around the bottom of the candles with some length to spare. Purifying herbs or incense such as rose or lavender. Table to use as an altar. Matches.

Optional: Small drawstring bags. Heart-shaped stones or candy or anything else appropriate. Small pieces of chocolate.

To arrange the ritual: Place all supplies on the table. Pass out candles and spells.

• • •

Pass the purifying herbs/incense around the table. Each person can waft the smoke over themselves, spending extra time over the heart area. Leader can say, "With this blessed smoke, we waft away all the negativity of our daily lives and enter into sacred space clean and clear and ready for magical work."

If desired, you can do a formal circle casting now, call the quarters, and invoke the Goddess or God and Goddess.

Spend a little time talking about what love means to each of you. Go around the circle and discuss what kinds of love you have and what love you feel is missing from your lives. Remember, in this area especially, to refrain from being judgmental.

Spend some time writing down the ways in which you would like to have more love in your life. You can choose one or many.

Each person should fold their piece of paper into a narrow strip and use a ribbon to tie it around the bottom of their candle. Tie off the ribbon with three or nine knots since those are both powerful magical numbers. Either place the stone in front of the candle or tie it on with the ribbon too.

Pass the rose petals or lavender around the table so each person can sprinkle the herbs around the base of their candle, onto the plate it is sitting on.

Take a moment of silence for everyone to focus on their intentions, then everyone should light their candles and recite the spell together.

Love as a blessing
Grows like a flower
Stronger and brighter
With each passing hour
Love as a gift
Sent from above
I trust in the gods
To send me sweet love
Love I deserve
And love I desire
Let love come to me
With these herbs and this fire
Love as a blessing
Love as a gift
Send me love that will comfort
And love that will lift
So mote it be!

Sit for another moment in silence, watching the flames of the candles burn, then snuff them out. If you want, you can scoop the herbs and the stone into a small bag, and take the candles home and light them for a few moments every day (with or without repeating the spell).

If you called the quarters and invoked the Goddess, dismiss the quarters now and thank the Goddess.

To open the circle, you can say, "Merry meet, merry part, and merry meet again."

Banishing

Unlike many other rituals that are best performed on the full moon, banishing rituals lend themselves well to the night of the dark moon, when the moon isn't visible at all. Alternately, they can be done right after the full moon, as the moon is waning, to tap into the diminishing power of the moon's energy.

Banishing magic is a delicate balancing act. You don't want to put out anything negative, but at the same time, if there is something (or someone) you need to get rid of for your own health and well-being, that is a positive thing. This is a simple ritual that should work for anything from banishing your own bad habits to blocking the influence of those who mean you harm. Doing this ritual with a coven will only strengthen the magic each of you puts out.

Supplies: Black votive candles, one for each person. Toothpicks. Purifying herbs or incense. Matches. Table to use as an altar. Copies of the spell. Matches.

Optional: If you can have a bonfire or a firesafe container outside, you can also use paper and pens.

To arrange the ritual: Each person should be given a candle, a toothpick (or they can use some sharp instrument of their own, such as an athame), and a copy of the spell. If you are using a bonfire, have it started before the ritual begins and hand out paper and pens.

• • •

Pass the herbs/incense around the circle to the left. The leader can say, "With this blessed smoke, we waft away all the negativity of our daily lives and enter into sacred space clean and clear and ready for magical work." Because of the kind of magical work you are about to do, be sure to take your time and really concentrate on clearing yourself of anything that might get in the way of what you wish to achieve.

If desired, you can do a formal circle casting, call the quarters, and invoke the Goddess. Otherwise you can cast the circle hand to hand, and the leader can say, "The circle is cast; we are between the worlds in a safe and protected space."

The leader says, "No matter how hard we try, there are always things in our lives that stand in the way of our forward movement and our happiness. Sometimes those things come from outside of us: bad influences, people who don't have our best interests at heart, jobs that suck our energy without giving anything in return. Sometimes they come from within: unproductive or destructive habits, old memories or patterns that drag us down, lack of willpower or self-confidence. Tonight we will work together to banish from our lives all those things that no longer work for our benefit. Take your candle and etch into it the names of anything you wish to banish from your life. Take some time to really think about your choices. Once banished, it is often difficult or impossible to get something back, so make sure you really want to be rid of whatever it is. If you're not sure, it is always okay to write something like 'unhappiness' or 'stress,' no matter what is causing them."

NOTE: If using a bonfire, also have people write the same words on their pieces of paper.

Have everyone take some time to think about what they wish to banish and etch it onto their candles. This is a time for focus and inward contemplation, not chat.

When everyone is ready, have them light their candles, then recite the spell together.

Banish stress and banish sorrow
Banish anger unproductive
Banish fear about tomorrow
And all habits too destructive
Banish those who mean us harm
Banish that which blocks our way
With our magic and its charm
Let all these things be gone to stay!

Blow out the candles all at once. If using a bonfire, throw in the pieces of paper now.

Take a moment of silence, then pass the herbs/incense again, concentrating on clearing away any remnants of whatever it is you got rid of. The candles can be taken home and burned every night for a month or until the next dark or full moon, depending on when you did the ritual.

If you did a formal circle casting, dismiss the quarters and thank the Goddess. Otherwise, simply say, "The circle is open but never broken. Merry meet, merry part, and merry meet again."

Section 9

Spirit and Divination

There are some practices that are less about ritual and more about working with spirit or intuition. There might be some formal ritual aspects, such as cleansing or protection, or you might just choose to perform these with nothing more than mindful appreciation of being in sacred space doing magical work.

Most of these can be performed at any time, although the full moon is an especially powerful period for this kind of magic. Divination is also often done on the summer solstice and on Samhain, when the boundaries between our world and the world that lies beyond are said to be at their thinnest.

Back-to-Back Heart Meditation

Written by my friend Lisa, who I talked about in section 3, this was designed for a two-person coven, but you can also adapt it to use as a guided meditation for a large group, as long as you have an even number of people plus one person facilitating.

> "Sit back-to-back with your spines and skulls gently touching. This is an exercise in support, not in leaning. It may take both of you a few minutes to get strongly centered in your own being and rooted to the ground. When you are ready, you can gently, slightly recline until your bodies meet. Bring your attention to your own breath first, breathing deeply and slowly but softly. Once you're attuned to your breath, begin noticing the other's.

Do not try to synchronize; simply notice your breath while also noticing their breath. If synchronization happens naturally and you feel it, don't get attached.

"When you're fully relaxed, bring your attention to your heart, feeling its energy, allowing it to open and expand, recognizing that as it does, it radiates to all sides, a glowing sphere of beautiful emerald light. As it radiates through your back, it merges with the heart-light flowing from your partner's back—a tangible connection that represents the deeper truth: We are not separate. We are all part of each other, part of the Goddess and God, the Universe, the One.

"When you feel grounded, relaxed, and connected with your partner, take a few deep breaths, slowly separating, and begin the rest of your ritual, if you are doing something additional."

Tea Ceremony for Two

Tea is a wonderful drink. Herbal tea in particular lends itself well to magical work because there are many herbs that have both medicinal and magical properties as well as taste delicious (although not everyone likes the taste of every herb, of course, and as with any plant, you will want to be mindful of allergies). You can do this simple magical tea ceremony with any herb that is safe to consume—not all are—and use either just one or a few different kinds. This can also work well for a small group.

Here are a few of my favorite herbs to make tea out of. Some of these have multiple associations, so they are extra handy to have around.

Chamomile—This herb is the go-to for peace, sleep, love, and prosperity. I also find it useful in healing mixes because of the peace and calm it can bring.

Ginger—This heat-producing root is good for energy, power, prosperity, success, and love (especially the passionate kind).

Lemon—You might not think of lemon as an herb, but dried lemon peel can be added to herbal tea mixes with ease, and it excels at purification, cleansing, love, and energy. You can also add a few drops of fresh lemon to zing up any tea.

Lemon Balm—An easy-to-grow member of the mint family, this herb is sacred to the goddesses Artemis and Diana. Both medically and magically, it is good for calm, sleep, anxiety, and healing, and it is also used in magic for happiness and love.

Peppermint—A healing herb traditionally used to soothe digestion and ease headaches, peppermint is used magically for healing, purification, love, prosperity, abundance, and to increase psychic powers. Even the scent of the brewing tea can lift your spirits.

Rose—You can use dried rose petals in tea, but for an extra boost of healing (and vitamin C), try rose hips, which are the fruit of the plant. Usually associated with love, rose is also good for healing, protection, and divination.

Rosemary—Rosemary is a sharp-tasting herb you might not want to make a strong tea out of, but a little bit added to other herbs will boost any work toward healing, protection, love, mental sharpness, memory, and purification.

There are plenty of other herbs that can be added to teas for magical work. If you have a favorite, it might be worth checking to see if it has specific magical associations.

Start by choosing the magical goal for your ritual, and then pick the herbs that you will use for your tea.

Supplies: Herbs of your choice (at least a teaspoon of each or more as desired). A teapot to brew the tea in (if this is a ritual you will do often, you may want to buy a special teapot for magical use; otherwise, any teapot will do). Two small mugs or heatproof cups. A tea ball (if you have never used one, they hold loose tea and are placed inside the pot to steep). A container of not-quite-boiling water. Large candle in white or a color that symbolizes the work you are doing, such as blue for healing. Purifying herbs or incense. Matches.

Optional: Items to symbolize your magical goal. Honey if you don't like the taste of the herbs without it (bees are sacred to the Goddess). A bell, chimes, or a gong if you have one.

NOTE: This is a quiet and peaceful ritual. If possible, sit someplace where you won't be disturbed by outside noises and see how slowly and calmly you can do this.

• • •

Set out all your tools and sit opposite your magical partner across a table or next to each other with a small table between you.

Light the herbs or incense and waft the smoke over your magical supplies, saying, "Bless these herbs and the work we do with them." Leave the herbs or incense smoldering in a firesafe container if you like.

Moving slowly and mindfully, and focusing on the magical intention you will be working toward, place the herb or herbs in the tea ball and put it into the teapot, making sure you hold on to the chain or stick at the other end. With two people, you can take turns doing each step or each do a part of it (one of you adding some herbs and the other adding more, for instance, or one of you doing the incense and the other loading the tea ball). Pour the hot water over the herbs. (Add honey now if desired.) Holding the end of the tea ball, swirl the herbs inside the pot nine times clockwise, then place the cover on the teapot to let the herbs steep for as long as necessary. Loose herbs and flowers usually take a few minutes, and tougher roots like ginger may take ten minutes or more. As it steeps, focus on your magical goal.

Together or taking turns, each of you can ring a bell or chime if you have one or simply clap your hands quietly three times over the top of the teapot and say, "Herbs into tea; nature's sweet alchemy. Our magic is done; so mote it be."

Pour some tea into your companion's cup and have them pour some into yours. Sip slowly, focusing on your magical goal as if its potential was entering your body with every sip.

When you are done, you can gently click your cups together or raise them in the air in each other's direction. If you are outside, you can pour out any remaining tea onto the ground or you may let it cool and each keep a small container to drink later.

Unity Ritual

This is a simple and yet surprisingly powerful ritual designed to be done with a large group of people. It can be done with a smaller group, but it may not resonate quite so strongly. It can be led by one person or two or three who each lead one section of the ritual. There are no supplies needed, so it is perfect for if you just want to keep things simple or if you'll be in a setting where candles and burning herbs can't be used

(I originally created this to use at a Pagan convention held at a hotel, where open flames and smoke weren't allowed).

• • •

Start by having everyone stand in a circle. If there are people who can't stand, it is fine to provide seating.

To cast the circle, the leader says, "We cast this circle with the voice of unity and in the spirit of unity. Say it with me: The circle is cast." All repeat together: "The circle is cast!"

The leader will call the quarters through a call and response approach, which means they say the first part and the entire group utters the response together. It is usually best to have the ritual leader explain this ahead of time if those taking part haven't worked together regularly. It can also be helpful to have a few people prepared to start the response so everyone gets the idea, or to hand the call and response words out to participants when they arrive. This should be done with energy and enthusiasm. The response can even be shouted, if you want. The group can stay facing inward or else turn to face each quarter.

Call and response quarter call:

East—Call (leader): "Who breaths air?"

Response (all): "We all breathe the air!"

South—Call (leader) "Who feels love and passion?"

Response (all): "We all feel love and passion!"

West—Call (leader): "Who is made of water?"

Response: "We are all made of water!"

North—Call (leader): "Who comes from the earth?"

Response: "We all come from the earth!"

Spirit—Call (leader): "Who is filled with spirit?"

Response: "We are all filled with spirit!"

Leader: "And so we invite the presence of spirit to join us in our rite."

Response: "So mote it be."

Leader or other member: "We will now send energy around the room with a gentle touch on the arm or shoulder of the person next to you, one by one. If you don't wish to be touched, put your hand out with the palm up, and the person next to you can simply hold their hand palm down over yours from about 2 inches away. Send a feeling of love and unity around the room until we are all connected." The leader starts by sending loving energy to the person on their left, and this continues around the circle until it returns to where it started. This should be done in relative silence, with as much focus as people can manage.

Leader or other member: "Now we are going to send a series of words around the room in the same fashion, starting with one person and then adding everyone else one by one. Keep repeating the first word until everyone in the room is saying it, then we'll change. When we get to the word 'one,' I'll raise my arms and we'll all send the energy out into the universe. When I finish with the last OM, put your hands over your heart and take the energy in." The first word is repeated until all are saying it, then the leader starts the next word, and so on.

OM

I am

we are

human

sacred

united

One (send out into universe by raising hands in the air)

OM (hands over heart, take into self)

Stand in silence for a few moments.

Leader: "I thank the quarters for guarding our circle. I thank the gods for watching over us. And I thank you all for joining me in this powerful ritual for unity. May the energy we created together continue to grow and flourish in the days to come. So mote it be!"

All: "So mote it be."

Guided Meditation, Drumming, and Chanting

One of the easiest rituals to do with a gathering of loosely associated witches is one that involves drumming and chanting. Adding a simple guided meditation to this will lift it to another level. If you can, this is a great ritual to do under a full moon outside, although it can be done any time and in any place where there is enough room for all those taking part to gather. Be sure to tell people ahead of time to bring a drum if they have one (or any other rhythm instrument, like a rattle), and try to have people bring extras for those who don't own one.

Supplies: Drums or rattles. If you're not good at spontaneously coming up with a guided meditation, it is good to have one written down ahead or bring a copy of this one. (If you're doing this outside in the dark, you might need a flashlight.)

• • •

Gather everyone in a circle and explain what you'll be doing. Hand out extra instruments as needed. If there are people who don't have one, they can clap, stomp their feet, or simply groove on what everyone else is doing. If you happen to have one person who is good at keeping a regular beat, it can help to have them start things off. Otherwise, just start with a slow, steady beat.

Tell people they can close their eyes if they want to and take a few slow, deep breaths. Then start with your own guided meditation or read this one:

"Hear the drum beating. It is the echo of the earth's heartbeat far below us. Focus on where your feet meet the ground. Send your awareness down through the soles of your feet, down, down, down below the surface of the land. Down through the dirt, through the layers of years, as if you could send out roots like a tree, connecting with the earth below, down to the fire at its core. Feel the pulse of the dancing flames, the heartbeat of the earth. Then bring your awareness back up through your own center, pausing for a moment to feel the energy there, then moving upward. Up through your heart, up through the top of your head, sending your awareness up toward the sky, toward the vibrant sun that gives us all life and the moon with her magic. Feel the pulse of the universe, the rhythm of the sky, and bring it back down with you to meet that heartbeat of the earth. Feel your own heartbeat echoing in your bones. You are the sky. You are the earth. You are energy and magic. You are the beat of the drum. *Ahhhhh.* Breathe out and return to this reality, stronger and more in touch with all that lies above and below."

Drum for a few minutes in silence and then start the chant. If you aren't familiar with it, you can find examples online so you can lead others in it as it does have something of a tune to it. This one is very simple. If you have another chant you prefer, you can substitute it instead.

"Air I am, fire I am, water, earth, and spirit I am." Repeat until energy builds and then drum loudly at the end, when the leader will purposely drum louder and then give one big thump to signal the drumming is over. The energy can be sent out into the universe or taken inside by the participants or both.

You may want to suggest that people ground all the energy they've built up by reaching down and putting their hands on the ground. Otherwise they may end up feeling buzzy and wired.

Divination with Tarot

—for two—

Divination work is fun to do within a group setting. Blue Moon Circle often pulls one tarot or oracle card, either for ourselves or the person next to us in the circle. We've also used rune stones on occasion. But it can be difficult to do anything more detailed when you have a number of people—it takes too long, it is hard to maintain focus, and not everyone feels comfortable doing a full reading for someone else.

In a two-person group, you are less likely to be dealing with these issues, so you can spend more time on divination as long as you are both into it. If you are beginners, this is the perfect way to practice. If you are more experienced, having someone to do divination with on a regular basis is a real bonus.

This particular tarot ritual is designed specifically for two. If you have a larger group, you can also break up into pairs and take turns reading for each other.

I like to do divination work on the new moon to see what lies ahead, on the full moon for the bigger picture issues, and on powerful days like the summer solstice or Samhain for general information the universe wants me to know. But really, there is no wrong time, and you can practice divination whenever you need it or are in the mood. When you're learning, it can be useful to do it often and write down each reading in a Book of Shadows or notebook. Don't worry if you need to refer to the book that came with your tarot deck or another reference book. It is good to listen to your instincts, but especially if you are just starting out, it is fine to look up the meanings of the cards if you are feeling unsure.

This ritual can be done with a quick three-card reading (past/present/future), a more detailed ten-card Celtic Cross layout, or any other format you and your magical partner both agree on. The approach is the same either way. I'll use the three-card reading for an example, but feel free to substitute whichever kind you feel like using.

Supplies: A tarot deck (if you each have your own, you can use both if you prefer). Two white candles. Purifying herbs or incense. Matches. A table where the two of you can sit opposite each other.

Optional: Books of Shadows or notebooks to write down your results in. Pens. A silk scarf or piece of silk to lay the cards on. Quiet background music or drumming. Cakes and ale for when you're done.

• • •

Place the candles on either side of the table so they won't get in the way. If you are using a piece of silk or some other cloth to lay the cards on, put it on the table in between you and your magical partner with the deck or decks stacked on top.

Light your purifying herbs or incense and waft it over the cards. Take turns lighting a candle and saying, "Goddess, please guide my thoughts and my intuition so that I might clearly see the answers before me."

Take a few moments to sit in silence (or with quiet background music playing) and think about the question or questions you want to ask.

If you are the person doing the reading, shuffle the deck you are using or have the person the reading is for shuffle and then hand the cards back. Have them split the deck into three stacks and then place them together in any order they choose, then say what their question is. You would then deal out three cards. You can do this one at a time, giving your interpretation of each card as it comes up, or place all three facedown and then turn them up one at a time. Do your best to answer the question, listening to your intuition. If you feel that there is something missing, you can have the other person pull a random card from the deck for clarification. Discuss what the reading has shown you.

> NOTE: When I read tarot, I shuffle the cards myself, in part because they can be awkward to handle for those who are not used to them and in part because I like to get the feel for the energy of the reading, but many tarot readers have the person they are reading for—called the querant—shuffle the cards for themselves. Either way is fine.

Then have the second person do a reading for the first in the same way.

When you are done, wave your purifying herbs or incense over your cards to cleanse them again and put them away. Have cakes and ale if desired, and jot down a few notes about the readings while they are still clear in your mind.

Divination with Oracle Cards

It can be a lot of fun to do divination for each other within a group setting, and unless your group is very large, you may choose to occasionally set aside some time to do tarot readings or other divination exchanges. The night of the full moon, the summer solstice, and Samhain are all great times for serious divination.

But there are also divination practices that don't require such a high level of time, energy, and concentration but are still fun and useful. One of the things Blue Moon Circle likes to do is integrate the use of oracle cards into some of our rituals. We pass whichever deck we are using around the circle and pick one random card each, either for ourselves or for the person sitting to our left.

The benefit of using oracle cards is that they tend to be simpler to interpret than tarot and usually have fewer cards in the deck. Many of them come with small booklets, although it is good practice to use your own intuition. We use my own *Everyday Witch Oracle* deck (with art by Elisabeth Alba), of course, but I also have a number of decks featuring goddesses, affirmations, and even cats. There are literally thousands of decks out there, and you can start with one or two that feel as though they would be the most in tune with you and your group.

Here are a few examples of the ones we use:

Blessed Be Cards: Mystical Celtic Blessings to Enrich & Empower—Lucy Cavendish, art by Jane Starr Weils

Conscious Spirit Oracle Deck—Kim Dreyer

Cosmic Cat Wisdom Cards—Randy Crutcher and Barb Horn

Gifts of the Goddess Affirmation Cards—Amy Zerner and Monte Farber

Goddess Inspiration Oracle—Kris Waldherr

Goddesses: Knowledge Cards—Michael Babcock, art by Susan Seddon Boulet

Journey to the Goddess Realm Oracle Deck—Lisa Porter

Peace Oracle: Guidance for Challenging Times—Toni Carmine Salerno and Leela J. Williams

Here is one example of a ritual using oracle cards. You can, of course, change it up to suit your group's needs at any given time.

Supplies: The oracle deck of your choice. Four quarter candles (yellow, red, blue, and green or all white/natural). Goddess candle (white or silver). Purifying herbs or incense.

Optional: Salt and water in a small dish. Quiet background music or drumming CD. Bell. Notebooks or Books of Shadows and pens to write down the divination result (it can be useful to keep track of these kinds of things). Bag or basket to hold the cards. Speaking stick. Cakes and ale.

To arrange the ritual: Set up your circle with the quarter candles at the four directions and the other supplies on a table or cloth in the middle of the circle. You will be sitting for much of this, so you may want cushions or chairs if people aren't comfortable sitting on the ground. This is a fairly casual and relaxed ritual.

• • •

Cast the circle hand to hand or in whatever way you usually do.

Light the purifying herbs or incense and pass it around your circle, giving each person a chance to cleanse themselves and the space around them. When the purifying herbs or incense return to the person who started it, they should waft it over the oracle cards as well.

If desired, pass the bowl of salt and water and have each member cleanse and purify themselves for the work ahead by anointing themselves at the third eye (middle of forehead), lips, heart, and center (bellybutton). Since you will be speaking, you might want to anoint the throat chakra as well.

Call the quarters by lighting each candle in turn, starting with east (this can be done by one person or different people). Say: "We call to the east, the power of air. Come join our circle bringing wisdom and the ability to speak it clearly. We call to the south, the power of fire. Come join our circle, bringing compassion and creativity that we can share with each other. We call to the west, the power of water. Come join our circle and help us go with the flow of whatever arises as we seek knowledge. We call to the north, the power of earth. Come join our circle and help us be grounded and wise. So mote it be."

Light the Goddess candle and invoke the Goddess or any specific goddess you choose. Say: "Great Goddess, we invite you to join us in our circle. Guide our hands and minds, lend us your wisdom and clarity, and help us learn those things that will be most useful to us today. Welcome, and blessed be."

The leader or a member should guide the group in a simple grounding exercise, which is helpful when doing any kind of divination work. They can use their own words or say: "Close your eyes. Take a few slow, deep breaths and feel yourself settle more deeply into sacred space. Visualize sending energy down through your feet and connecting with the ground below, strong and firm and stable. Now visualize sending energy up through the top of your head to the skies above, accessing the wisdom and serenity of the sky. Bring that energy back from above and below to meet at your core, grounding and centering you for the work ahead. Take another deep breath, open your eyes, and feel yourself focused and ready to access whatever knowledge the universe has to share with you."

Everyone should sit comfortably. If you will be playing music or drumming in the background, start it now.

Pass the cards around the table (you can leave them in their box, place them in a bag or basket, or simply pass the cards as a stack). Each person should take one card without looking at it.

Going around the circle one at a time, each person should look at the card they pulled and share what it says to them. You can use a general approach for the readings (What do we need to know today?) or something more specific, depending on the deck. If you are using a goddess deck, for instance, you may want to ask, "Which goddess can I learn something from today?"

If you want, you can then pass the deck a second time (after returning the first cards) and have people choose a card for the person next to them. If so, go around the circle again and this time have people interpret the card for the one they chose for. If desired, write the card results in notebooks or a Book of Shadows.

Pass cakes and ale (optional).

If you want, pass a speaking stick and have everyone talk about what they got from the messages they received.

Stand up. Thank the quarters for coming to your circle and for their help ("Thank you, powers of air, for attending our ritual" or something simple like that). Snuff out those candles.

Thank the Goddess for joining you in your circle and snuff out that candle.

Open the circle by saying, "The circle is open but never broken. Merry meet, merry part, and merry meet again."

Divination with Rune Stones

Rune stones are a form of divination that dates back to ancient times. The ones we most commonly use are the Norse/Germanic version known as the Elder Futhark. The twenty-five stones come from an alphabet of twenty-four letters plus one blank stone (Wyrd). Unlike tarot cards, which some people find difficult to master, the symbols on rune stones are relatively simple and easy to interpret (although if you aren't familiar with them, it can help to have a book handy, something I suggest for this ritual).

Rune stones can be made from any material, although wood, clay, and rock are probably the most common. You can easily make your own set if you don't want to buy one, but they also tend to be relatively inexpensive. If you work with a larger group of people, odds are that at least one person in that group has a set if you don't.

If using rune stones for more detailed divination work, you might spread all the runes facedown on a table, but for this ritual, you will want to have them in a drawstring bag that can be passed around the circle.

Supplies: Bag of rune stones. Rune book.

Optional: Purifying herbs or incense. Quarter candles. God/Goddess candles. Drums.

• • •

This can be done standing or sitting comfortably. You can cast a formal circle and call the quarters first if you want or spend some time drumming or chanting to raise energy. When you feel as though people are ready, give them the following instructions:

"Spend a few minutes thinking about a question you need answers to or a problem you could use some guidance on.

Fix that question firmly in your mind. Now we will pass the bag of rune stones around the circle. Each of us will pull a rune for the person standing to our left. So I will start by pulling a rune for the person standing next to me and say what it is out loud. We will pass a book along with the stones for anyone who isn't practiced at using them. Say what the rune is, then read aloud what the book says its meaning is. If they desire, the person you pulled the stone for can say whether or not the rune was a helpful answer to their question and what their question was, but it is okay to just keep that to yourself if you choose. Put the rune you picked back into the bag and shake it a few times to mix up the stones, then pass it to the next person. In this way, we will go around the entire circle."

Once everyone has had a turn, you can discuss the runes and whether or not they were helpful. If you have a relatively small gathering, you can send the bag around the circle a few times, either to answer different questions or get more clarity on a previous reading.

If you cast a formal circle and called the quarters, etc., dismiss the circle in the usual way.

CONCLUSION

I can honestly say that some of the best moments of my life have been those spent in circle with my fellow witches. This is especially true for rituals and feasts shared with my own coven, Blue Moon Circle, who have become closer than family, but I have also had amazing times with large groups at both local celebrations and faraway conventions as well as the coven where I got my initial introduction to Witchcraft.

While I value the magic I practice on my own, there is a special energy to be found when witches come together with a common purpose and open hearts. When everything works as it should, we can generate an amazing amount of power together for the good of all.

This isn't to say that all group work is wonderful. I have attended a few spectacular fails of rituals (although most of them were harmless and fairly humorous in retrospect). And while I have been fortunate enough to avoid the rare nasty and ill-intentioned coven leaders, there are some out there. As with anything else, always listen to your gut. If something seems off to you, listen to that inner wisdom and go elsewhere.

For the most part, though, gathering with other witches can be uplifting, energizing, and just plain fun. If you have gotten nothing else out of this book, I hope you have learned that the old rules no longer apply. You can find or create the coven that suits your needs, both magical and mundane.

Whether you gather with one other person or fifty, meet on the full moons or the sabbats, dress up in garb or wear jeans and a tee shirt, there is a coven out there with your name on it. And if there isn't, maybe it is time to start one of your own. If you do, by all means use this book as a starting point, but remember that you can change any of it to better fit your idea of what a coven is.

The only rules, really, are to respect the people you practice magic with, keep the lines of communication open, be clear about what is and isn't okay, and approach your shared practice with an open mind and an open heart. It is said that witches worship the gods with both reverence and mirth. Don't forget to have fun, but also treat your practice seriously and the gods with the reverence they deserve.

And as it says at the end of the Wiccan Rede, "Follow this with mind and heart, and merry ye meet, and merry ye part."

Until we meet again,

blessed be.

Deborah Blake

appendix

Common Terms

There are a few words and terms that are used in the practice of Witchcraft that may be unfamiliar to you if you are just beginning to walk this path. You might even have come across a few so far while you were reading this book. You can, of course, always look things up online or elsewhere, but for ease of use, here are a few of the most basic ones.

Banishing—Banishing means to get rid of something. In magic, this can be physical (health issues, addiction), psychological (depression, bad habits, repeating patterns that don't work for you anymore), spiritual (dark energies, although it can be difficult to tell if such things are coming from the inside or the outside), or even people. Be very careful if you use magic to banish someone from your life—it is almost always permanent, and you may not get a chance to change your mind. When groups do banishing work together, it is usually of a more general nature. For instance, everyone may write down things they want to banish from their lives and take turns throwing the slips of paper into the Samhain bonfire.

Blessing—We often talk about blessing and consecrating new tools or a space being used for magical work. Essentially this is asking the Goddess and God (or whatever you want to call deity) to send their blessings. This adds a level of power and spirit to whatever or whoever (like a new baby) is being blessed.

Cakes and Ale—This is a part of the ritual where some form of food and drink are passed around the circle, usually coming right before the end, after all the serious magical work is done. It serves to ground the participants back to the real world and is also symbolic of the bonds we share as witches. If you have guests that you don't know well or if there are participants under the legal age for drinking, it is best to stick to nonalcoholic "ale." If your group includes someone with alcohol issues, you will always want to use juice or water. Cider makes for a nice substitute, especially in the fall. We also like pomegranate juice, which is rich and beautiful and associated with the goddess Persephone.

Charge of the Goddess—A traditional Wiccan poem that is sometimes recited as part of ritual, usually at the beginning, but not always. It can be extremely powerful and moving. There is a less commonly used Charge of the God that was written later.

Cleansing and Clearing—We talk about this a lot. In magical work, cleansing isn't about practical physical cleaning but rather clearing the energy of people or places or things. You might cleanse the circle before you start a ritual or use a new tool, especially if it previously belonged to someone and you want to rid it of any leftover energy. When I moved into my house, I had my group come over and cleanse the house from top to bottom, not because if felt bad, but simply to wash away the energy of the previous occupant so I could make it completely my own. Then we did a house blessing.

Consecrate—Consecrating is related to blessing, but it is more that we are pledging whatever is being consecrated (a new tool, a charm bag, a tarot deck) to positive magical use.

Dedication—Dedication is usually the act of making a formal commitment, either to a coven or to the gods. Some groups ask new members to do a dedication after a year and a day, others only want people to do it when they feel ready, and some (like mine and other eclectic covens) don't necessarily do dedications at all. We actually did a group dedication together when we founded Blue Moon Circle, but we haven't had any individual ones for people who joined later. Witches may also do a dedication to the gods in general or one deity in particular. When I became a high priestess, I did a very small personal dedication in which I pledged my service to the gods and my fellow witches.

Deity—A general word for any god or goddess.

Deosil—Movement done in a clockwise direction, sometimes for increase or positive work or to close a circle. Almost all movement within a magical circle is done in a deosil fashion, even if this means walking all the way around the circle to get back to where you started. This is traditional, but you don't have to follow this if you choose not to.

Divination—Divination is a way of looking for answers or for knowledge of the future. It can involve a number of different tools, including tarot cards, rune stones, oracle cards, scrying, and more. It comes from a Latin word that means "to foresee, to foretell, to predict" and is actually related to the word *divine*, which suggests that this knowledge may come from the gods.

Eclectic Witch—An eclectic witch is one who takes elements of different Witchcraft approaches (and occasionally other spiritual paths) and combines them into a practice that works for them. For instance, I use bits and pieces from the Wiccan style of Witchcraft I was first taught, some more traditional older Witchcraft practices, kitchen witchery, green Witchcraft, and even the Zen Buddhism I studied before becoming a witch.

Element—This is a term generally applied to the four elements of earth, air, fire, and water. They are also referred to as elemental powers. Spirit is sometimes considered to be a fifth element and the most important of all.

Esbats—The lunar rituals and observances that take place at the full moon or the new moon.

Garb—Ritual clothing.

Handfasting—A Pagan wedding rite. This may be a formal legal ceremony or a ritual that is spiritually but not legally binding. Some are done for a year and a day and others are for life, as any other wedding would be. The term comes from "hand fastening" because the couple is often loosely bound together with a cord during the ceremony to symbolize that they are binding themselves together as one.

High priest/high priestess—A Pagan spiritual leader, usually someone who has had years of experience and practice before assuming the title. This is more of a Wiccan term than a general Witchcraft one, although it can vary from group to group. Technically, I am the high priestess of Blue Moon Circle, but I don't even really use the term anymore. In traditional Wicca, one usually moved through three levels of training before becoming a high priest or high priestess. The position comes with a certain responsibility, not just to one's own group but also to the Pagan community at large (think of it as being a minister), and it is not something to be undertaken lightly.

Hiving off—A traditional Wiccan term used when a member of a coven becomes a high priest or high priestess and leaves to start their own coven.

Intent—The purpose of a spell or magical working; also the focused energy used to bring it about. Intent is one of the most important components of spell work. In order to be successful, you need to be clear about your intentions when casting a spell.

Invocation—An invocation is a call, a prayer, or a summoning. When we talk about invocations in Witchcraft, it is usually associated with inviting the elements or the deities to come into our magical space.

Law of Three—This is a generally accepted Wiccan precept that everything you put out into the universe comes back to you times three. So if you do positive magic, you will reap the rewards three times over, but if you do harmful magic, it will come back and bite you on the butt. Some people call this the Law of Returns, which is a bit simpler and basically means that what you put out is what you get back. I believe in this, and I've seen it happen, although it is true that you can look around and see a lot of people doing nasty things with seemingly no penalty. Still, for me, this concept lines up with my belief that it is important to be aware of what you are putting out into the world.

Maiden, Mother, and Crone—A few of the goddesses we worship in Witchcraft are triple goddesses of some kind or another, which means they manifest in three separate aspects. Hecate and Brigid are the prime examples of this. Maiden, Mother, and Crone are terms associated with the three different stages of a woman's life (essentially before, during, and after a woman's ability to have a child, but not necessarily tied to exact physical timetables), and in more traditional Wiccan forms of practice, they might be roles in a group or ritual. They are also tied to the different stages of the lunar cycle: waxing, full, and waning.

Mundane—This isn't an insult in any way. It is just the word some people use to indicate the part of their life that isn't magical. So I have my mundane friends and my witchy friends, for example. Since the advent of the Harry Potter books, some witches have adopted the term "muggle" instead, but that isn't as common.

Old Gods—Some witches use this term to refer to any pre-Christianity deities. So you might say that you worship the Old Gods if someone asks what religious path you follow.

Pagan—Someone who worships the Old Gods (almost always including at least one goddess) and follows a nature-based religion. Not all Pagans are witches, but all witches are Pagans. *Pagan* comes from a word that meant "dweller in the country" and referred to the fact that the rural folks in Europe were the last ones to be absorbed by the new Christian religion. I refer to myself equally as a Pagan and a witch, but there are definitely Pagans who are not witches and who would be insulted if you assumed they were.

Pentacle—A commonly used Witchcraft symbol that consists of a five-pointed star with a circle around it. The five points represent the five elements: earth, air, fire, water, and spirit, and the circle is the universe that holds them all, or unity. A pentagram, which is closely related to the pentacle, is a five-pointed star drawn in one continuous line. It is also used by witches but has shown up historically in many other cultures and religions. A pentacle is often used for protection as well as to symbolize Witchcraft.

Quarter—We talk a lot about the four quarters. These are directions used in magical work, and there are four, each with their own set of associations: east (air), south (fire), west (water), and north (earth).

Quarter calls—These are the invocations we say to invite the powers of the quarters to enter our sacred space. They may be as simple as "Powers of east, the element of air, please join me in my circle" or be considerably more elaborate. They should always be said with respect.

Sabbat—One of eight holidays in the Pagan calendar, which includes the two solstices, two equinoxes, and four quarter-cross holidays that fall at equal times between them. They are Imbolc (February 2), Ostara (spring equinox, around March 21), Beltane (May 1), Midsummer (summer solstice, around June 21), Lammas (August 2), Mabon (autumn equinox, around September 21), Samhain (October 31), and Yule (winter solstice, around December 21). The dates of the solstices and equinoxes vary slightly every year.

Solitary—A witch who practices alone rather than with a group. Most witches who belong to a coven also do solitary work, but a solitary witch is one who always or almost always practices on their own.

Speaking stick—A stick or some other object (this can be anything from a rock to a goblet) that is passed around the circle during ritual. Usually used at the end, it allows each participant to have a moment to speak without interruption about what is in their heart.

Wheel of the Year—The Pagan calendar of holidays and the turning of the seasons. Magical work is often done according to where on the Wheel of the Year we are, since the energy of the earth changes with the seasons. So magic for new starts might be done at the spring equinox, while magic for letting go might be done at Samhain, the last of the three harvest festivals.

Wicca—A specific modern form of Witchcraft practice brought over from England in the 1940s. It has since splintered off into many different variations, none of which follow exactly the same beliefs or tenets. The original Wiccan practices usually involved initiation into at least three levels and ornate formal rituals. All Wiccans are witches, but not all witches are Wiccans.

Wiccan Rede—The longer form is an elaborate poem written in archaic language by Doreen Valiente, sometimes called "the Mother of Modern Witchcraft." It was often used in the early days during ritual, and it spells out the rules of Wicca as they were when the practice began. The shorter form—"An' it harm none, do as ye will"—is often considered the Golden Rule of Wicca. It is followed by some witches but not all and basically means that you can do what you please as long as you aren't hurting anyone. Since that also includes yourself, the concept is more complicated than it seems on the surface.

Widdershins—Movement that is done in a counterclockwise direction, usually used for banishing, unbinding, or opening a magical circle at the end of a ritual.

Ritual Etiquette

While it is true that Witchcraft has very few hard-and-fast rules—and that even those may be a matter of personal choice—there are a few issues of basic ritual etiquette that are usually observed when working with a group. If your coven decides not to follow one or more of these, that's fine, but until you have had a discussion about it—or if you are a guest at some other coven's ritual—it is best to stick to these unless told otherwise.

This particular list dates back to the founding of Blue Moon Circle, and therefore can be found in most of my books that talk about rituals. They were originally published in my first book, *Circle, Coven & Grove: A Year of Magickal Practice* (Llewellyn, 2007).

- **Whenever you move around the circle, go in a clockwise direction (deosil).** The only exception is when you are doing banishing work, in which case you walk counterclockwise (widdershins).
- **Once the circle is cast, it should not be broken**. Once cast, the circle exists outside of time and space, and it is a safe and sacred place. If you need to leave the circle space for any reason, you need to have someone "cut you out." This is done by drawing a doorway with an athame or your finger, starting at the ground and going up and over and then down again. To cut someone back into the circle, draw the doorway in reverse.
- **Never touch another witch's tools without permission**.
- **It is important to keep focus and concentration; there should be no chitchat during the main part of the ritual**. Informal talking is okay during certain situations that require less intense focus, such as some of the craft project sections.

- **Everything that is said in circle stays in circle**. It is crucial that the circle remain a safe place in which all those in attendance feel free to speak what is in their hearts. This means that nothing said in confidence may ever be repeated. This also means that you should never tell anyone outside of the circle any specifics of what occurred within, including the names of those who have attended ritual. Not everyone is out of the broom closet, and some people would rather not have others know they practice Witchcraft. This is one of the reasons that some witches use Craft names instead of real ones.
- **When the speaking stick is passed, only the person holding the stick may speak**. You will get your turn to talk when the stick comes around the circle. Be respectful of others and give your entire attention to whomever has the stick.
- **Show respect for the gods and the elements by standing during quarter calls and invocations and turning with the rest of the circle to face the appropriate directions.** If you do not know what to do, you should just copy everyone else. If you are physically unable to stand, that's fine. The gods will understand.
- **Show respect for the others in the circle.** Do not say negative things to others about those with whom you practice. Try not to judge or criticize. After all, you wouldn't want others to judge you.
- **Come to circle cleansed and prepared to do magickal work.** It is proper to bathe before rituals if at all possible. Never wear perfumes or colognes as many people are allergic or find the strong scents distracting. If your coven

dresses up, wear appropriate garb. Garb is any clothing you keep for magickal work—usually robes, fancy dresses, or cloaks. If you do not have garb, at least dress neatly.

- **Never come to circle under the influence of drugs or alcohol.** This is disrespectful to both the gods and your fellow circle members, and it makes it next to impossible to build up energy in any productive way.
- **Do not ask personal questions of those participants whom you do not know well.** This is the privacy issue again. People will volunteer information (like where they work) when they are ready.
- **Respect the gender identity of those within the group**. If someone asks to be referred to by an alternative pronoun or they/them, do your best to do so. If you mess up and forget, just apologize and try to remember the next time. Witchcraft is a welcoming and nonjudgmental religion, and the God and Goddess accept all who come to them.

Recommended Reading

Goddesses

Auset, Brandi. *The Goddess Guide: Exploring the Attributes and Correspondences of the Divine Feminine.* Woodbury: Llewellyn, 2009.

Illes, Judika. *Encyclopedia of Witchcraft: The Complete A–Z for the Entire Magical World.* London: HarperElement, 2005.

Jordan, Michael. *Encyclopedia of Gods: Over 2,500 Deities of the World.* New York: Facts on File, 1993.

Loar, Julie. *Goddesses for Every Day: Exploring the Wisdom & Power of the Divine Feminine Around the World.* Novato, CA: New World Library, 2008, 2011.

Monaghan, Patricia. *Encyclopedia of Goddesses & Heroines.* Novato, CA: New World Library, 2014.

———. *The Goddess Path: Myths, Invocations & Rituals.* St. Paul: Llewellyn, 1999.

Sky, Michelle. *Goddess Alive! Inviting Celtic & Norse Goddesses into Your Life.* Woodbury: Llewellyn, 2007.

———. *Goddess Aloud! Transforming Your World Through Rituals & Mantras.* Woodbury: Llewellyn, 2010.

Telesco, Patricia. *365 Goddess: A Daily Guide to the Magic and Inspiration of the Goddess.* New York: HarperOne, 1998.

Witchcraft Basics and General Practice

Blake, Deborah. *The Everyday Witch A to Z: An Amusing, Inspiring & Informative Guide to the Wonderful World of Witchcraft*. Woodbury: Llewellyn, 2008.

———. *A Year and a Day of Everyday Witchcraft: 366 Ways to Witchify Your Life*. Woodbury: Llewellyn, 2017.

———. *The Little Book of Cat Magic: Spells, Charms & Tales*. Woodbury: Llewellyn, 2018.

Buckland, Raymond. *Buckland's Complete Book of Witchcraft*. St. Paul: Llewellyn, 2002.

———. *Wicca for Life: The Way of the Craft—From Birth to Summerland*. New York: Citadel Press, 2001.

Cunningham, Scott. *Wicca: A Guide for the Solitary Practitioner*. St. Paul: Llewellyn, 1988.

Dubats, Sally. *Natural Magick*. New York: Citadel, 2002.

Grimassi, Raven. *Spirit of the Witch: Religion & Spirituality in Contemporary Witchcraft*. St. Paul: Llewellyn, 2003.

Holland, Eileen. *The Wicca Handbook*. York Beach, ME: Samuel Weiser, 2000.

McCoy, Edain. *The Witch's Coven: Finding or Forming Your Own Circle*. St. Paul: Llewellyn, 2003.

Seville, Christine. *Practical Wicca the Easy Way: Spells and Rituals to Heal and Harmonize Your Life*. New York: Sterling, 2003.

Trobe, Kala. *The Witch's Guide to Life*. St. Paul: Llewellyn, 2003.

Tuitéan, Paul, and Estelle Daniels. *Pocket Guide to Wicca*. Freedom, CA: Crossing Press, 1998.

Herbs

Cunningham, Scott. *The Complete Book of Incense, Oils & Brews.* St. Paul: Llewellyn, 1989.

———. *Cunningham's Encyclopedia of Magical Herbs.* St. Paul: Llewellyn, 1985.

———. *Magical Herbalism.* St. Paul: Llewellyn, 1982.

Dugan, Ellen. *Cottage Witchery: Natural Magick for Hearth and Home.* St. Paul: Llewellyn, 2005.

———. *Garden Witchery: Magick from the Ground Up.* St. Paul: Llewellyn, 2003.

Dunwich, Gerina. *The Wicca Garden: A Modern Witch's Book of Magickal and Enchanted Herbs and Plants.* Secaucus, NJ: Carol Publishing Group, 1996.

Morrison, Dorothy. *Bud, Blossom, & Leaf: The Magical Herb Gardener's Handbook.* St. Paul: Llewellyn, 2001.

Gemstones

Chase, Pamela Louise, and Jonathan Pawlik. *Healing with Gemstones.* Franklin Lakes, NJ: New Page, 2002.

Cunningham, Scott. *Cunningham's Encyclopedia of Crystal, Gem & Metal Magic.* St. Paul: Llewellyn, 1988.

Rituals & Spellcasting

Barrette, Elizabeth. *Composing Magic: How to Create Magical Spells, Rituals, Blessings, Chants, and Prayer.* Franklin Lakes, NJ: New Page, 2007.

Blake, Deborah. *Circle, Coven & Grove: A Year of Magickal Practice.* Woodbury: Llewellyn, 2007.

———. *Everyday Witch A to Z Spellbook: Wonderfully Witchy Blessings, Charms & Spells.* Woodbury: Llewellyn, 2010.

———. *Everyday Witch Book of Rituals: All You Need for a Magickal Year.* Woodbury: Llewellyn, 2012.

Connor, Kerri. *The Pocket Spell Creator: Magickal References at Your Fingertips.* Franklin Lakes, NJ: New Page Books, 2003.

Dugan, Ellen. *The Enchanted Cat: Feline Fascinations, Spells & Magick.* Woodbury: Llewellyn, 2006.

Galenorn, Yasmine. *Embracing the Moon: A Witch's Guide to Ritual Spellcraft and Shadow Work.* St. Paul: Llewellyn, 1998.

Hardie, Titania. *Titania's Magical Compendium: Spells and Rituals to Bring a Little Magic into Your Life.* San Diego: Thunder Bay, 2003.

Johnstone, Michael. *The Ultimate Encyclopedia of Spells: 88 Incantations to Entice Love, Improve a Career, Increase Wealth, Restore Health, and Spread Peace.* New York: Gramercy, 2003.

Nahmad, Claire. *Catspells: A Collection of Enchantments for You and Your Feline Companion.* Philadelphia: Running Press, 1993.

Renée, Janina. *By Candlelight: Rites for Celebration, Blessing & Prayer.* St. Paul: Llewellyn, 2004.

Telesco, Patricia. *Your Book of Shadows: How to Write Your Own Magickal Spells.* Secaucus, NJ : Carol Publishing, 1999.

West, Kate. *The Real Witches' Year: Spells, Rituals and Meditations for Every Day of the Year.* London: Element, 2004.

Wood, Gail. *Rituals of the Dark Moon: 13 Lunar Rites for a Magical Path.* St. Paul: Llewellyn, 2004.

Sabbats & Lunar Lore

Cole, Jennifer. *Ceremonies of the Seasons: Exploring and Celebrating Nature's Eternal Cycle.* London: Duncan Baird, 2007.

Dunwich, Gerina. *The Pagan Book of Halloween: A Complete Guide to the Magick, Incantations, Recipes, Spells, and Lore.* New York: Penguin Compass, 2000.

Green, Marion. *A Witch Alone: Thirteen Moons to Master Natural Magic.* London: Thorsons, 1991.

Kynes, Sandra. *A Year of Ritual: Sabbats & Esbats for Solitaries & Covens.* St. Paul: Llewellyn, 2004.

Morrison, Dorothy. *Everyday Moon Magic.* St. Paul: Llewellyn, 2003.

Ravenwolf, Silver. *Halloween: Customs, Recipes & Spells.* St. Paul: Llewellyn, 1999.

History, Classics & Traditional Practices

Adler, Margot. *Drawing Down the Moon: Witches, Druids, Goddess-Worshippers, and Other Pagans in America.* New York: Penguin, 2006.

Fitch, Ed. *Magical Rites from the Crystal Well: A Classic Text for Witches & Pagans.* St. Paul: Llewellyn, 1984.

Starhawk. *The Spiral Dance: A Rebirth of the Ancient Religion of the Great Goddess.* San Francisco: HarperSanFrancisco, 1999.

Telesco, Patricia, ed. *Cakes and Ale for the Pagan Soul: Spells, Recipes, and Reflections from Neopagan Elders and Teachers.* Berkeley, CA: Crossing Press, 2005.

Wildman, Laura, ed. *Celebrating the Pagan Soul: Our Own Stories of Inspiration and Community.* New York: Citadel, 2005.

Gods/Goddesses (Other)

Bolen, Jean Shinoda. *Goddesses in Older Women: Archetypes in Women Over Fifty.* New York: HarperCollins, 2001.

Wood, Gail. *The Wild God: Rituals and Meditations on the Sacred Masculine.* Niceville: Spilled Candy Books, 2006.

Personal Practices

Ardinger, Barbara. *Pagan Every Day: Finding the Extraordinary in Our Ordinary Lives.* San Francisco: Red Wheel/Weiser, 2006.

Blake, Deborah. *The Goddess Is in the Details: Wisdom for the Everyday Witch*. Woodbury: Llewellyn, 2009.

———. *Everyday Witchcraft: Making Time for Spirit in a Too-Busy World*. Woodbury: Llewellyn, 2015.

———. *The Eclectic Witch's Book of Shadows*. Woodbury: Llewellyn, 2021.

Curott, Phyllis. *Book of Shadows: A Modern Woman's Journey into the Wisdom of Witchcraft and the Magic of the Goddess*. New York: Broadway Books, 1998.

Digitalis, Raven. *Shadow Magick Compendium*. Woodbury: Llewellyn, 2008.

Dubats, Sally. *Natural Magick: The Essential Witch's Grimoire*. New York: Kensington, 1999.

Dumars, Denise. *Be Blessèd: Daily Devotions for Busy Wiccans and Pagans*. Franklin Lakes, NJ: New Page, 2006.

Eilers, Dana D. *The Practical Pagan: Commonsense Guidelines for Modern Practitioners*. Franklin Lakes, NJ: New Page, 2002.

Henes, Donna. *The Queen of My Self: Stepping into Sovereignty in Midlife*. Brooklyn: Monarch Press. 2005.

McCoy, Edain. *Spellworking for Covens: Magick for Two or More*. St. Paul: Llewellyn, 2002.

Moura, Ann. *Green Witchcraft: Folk Magic, Fairy Lore & Herb Craft*. St. Paul: Llewellyn, 1996.

Singer, Marion. *A Witch's 10 Commandments: Magickal Guidelines for Everyday Life*. Avon, MA: Provenance Press, 2006.

Sylvan, Dianne. *The Circle Within: Creating a Wiccan Spiritual Tradition*. St. Paul: Llewellyn, 2003.

Weinstein, Marion. *Positive Magic: Occult Self-Help*. New York: Earth Magic, 1994.

Correspondences & Reference

Greer, John Michael. *The New Encyclopedia of the Occult.* St. Paul: Llewellyn, 2003.

Grimassi, Raven. *Encyclopedia of Wicca & Witchcraft.* St. Paul: Llewellyn, 2000.

Guiley, Rosemary Ellen. *Encyclopedia of Magic and Alchemy.* New York: Facts On File, 2006.

———. *The Encyclopedia of Witches & Witchcraft: Second Edition.* New York: Facts On File, 1999.

Holland, Eileen. *Holland's Grimoire of Magickal Correspondences: A Ritual Handbook.* Franklin Lakes, NJ: New Page, 2006.

Illes, Judika. *Encyclopedia of Witchcraft: The Complete A–Z for the Entire Magical World.* London: HarperElement, 2005.

McColman, Carl. *The Well-Read Witch: Essential Books for Your Magickal Library.* Franklin Lakes, NJ: New Page, 2002.

Rosean, Lexa. *The Encyclopedia of Magickal Ingredients: A Wiccan Guide to Spellcasting.* New York: Pocket Books, 2005.

Advanced Learning

Bonewits, Isaac. *Real Magic: An Introductory Treatise on the Basic Principles of Yellow Magic.* Boston: Samuel Weiser, 1989.

Cunningham, Scott. *Earth, Air, Fire & Water: More Techniques of Natural Magic.* St. Paul: Llewellyn, 1991.

———. *Living Wicca: A Further Guide for the Solitary Practitioner.* St. Paul: Llewellyn, 1993.

de Angeles, Ly. *Witchcraft: Theory and Practice.* St. Paul: Llewellyn, 2000.

Penczak, Christopher. *The Mystic Foundation: Understanding & Exploring the Magical Universe.* Woodbury: Llewellyn, 2006.

Telesco, Patricia. *Advanced Wicca: Exploring Deeper Levels of Spiritual Skills and Masterful Magick*. New York: Citadel Press, 2000.

Weinstein, Marion. *Earth Magic: A Book of Shadows for Positive Witches*. Franklin Lakes, NJ: New Page, 2003.

• • •

In addition, I highly recommend the Llewellyn annuals, which have the advantage of giving you a taste of many different authors' writing. I often find people who are new to me and track down their books if they have written any. There is lots of varied wisdom in those pages. And I subscribe to *Witches and Pagans,* a Pagan magazine from BBI Media.

INDEX

To Write to the Author

If you wish to contact the author or would like more information about this book, please write to the author in care of Llewellyn Worldwide and we will forward your request. Both the author and the publisher appreciate hearing from you and learning of your enjoyment of this book and how it has helped you. Llewellyn Worldwide cannot guarantee that every letter written to the author can be answered, but all will be forwarded. Please write to:

Deborah Blake
℅ Llewellyn Worldwide
2143 Wooddale Drive
Woodbury, MN 55125–2989

Please enclose a self-addressed stamped envelope for reply
or $1.00 to cover costs. If outside the USA, enclose
an international postal reply coupon.

• • •

Many of Llewellyn's authors have websites with additional information and resources. For more information, please visit our website:

WWW.LLEWELLYN.COM